CONTEMPORARY'S

MATH SKILLS THAT WORK

A Functional Approach for Life and Work

BOOK ONE

ROBERT MITCHELL

Project Editors
Ellen Frechette
Kathy Osmus

Consultant
Janice Phillips
Workplace Literacy Instructor
William Rainey Harper College
Palatine, Illinois

CONTEMPORARY
BOOKS

CHICAGO

Photo Credits
Page viii: © Jim Whitmer. Page 14: © William Means, Tony
Stone Worldwide. Page 26: © Don Smetzer, Tony Stone
Worldwide. Page 58: © Jim Whitmer. Page 90: ©
Camerique, Inc. Page 128: © Barbara Filet, Tony Stone
Worldwide. Page 164: © Frank Cezus, Tony Stone
Worldwide.

Published by Contemporary Books, Inc.
Two Prudential Plaza, Chicago, Illinois 60601-6790
Manufactured in the United States of America
International Standard Book Number: 0-8092-4124-2

Editorial Director	*Production Assistant*
Caren Van Slyke	Marina Micari
Editorial	*Cover Design*
Karen Schenkenfelder	Georgene Sainati
Joe Carrig	
Lisa Dillman	*Illustrator*
Laura Larson	Cliff Hayes
Gerilee Hundt	
	Art & Production
Editorial Assistant	Carolyn Hopp
Erica Pochis	
	Typography
Editorial Production Manager	Impressions, Inc.
Norma Fioretti	Madison, Wisconsin

Cover photo © Allen Birnbach/Westlight

CONTENTS

To the Instructor

The Functional Approach to Math

Students often ask, "Why study math?" This is a fair question and one that is often difficult to answer convincingly in the classroom. As an instructor, you know that a student's perspective is quite different from your own. While you may see math as relevant in everyday life, many of your students regard math as something they'll never use again!

Part of our goal as math educators is to show why math is important and to do this in a way that draws students to the subject. We often ask ourselves, "How can I help my students form positive attitudes about math?"

Perhaps the best way to do this is to "make math real" by drawing on resources from your students' own experiences, resources familiar in their roles as family members, consumers, and employees. Emphasizing adult experiences is the cornerstone of the functional approach to math.

As a starting point, help adult students realize that recipes, rent payments, grocery bills, restaurant checks, phone and utility bills, checkbooks, charge cards, and dozens of other similar items are all mathematically rich topics. By using these familiar items as focal points, you can lay a groundwork of confidence and experience. Building upon these resources, you can give attention to higher-level computation and problem-solving skills as student interest and skill level increase. The functional approach to math prepares adults to use mathematics where they'll most likely need it: at home, in the marketplace, and at work.

About *Math Skills That Work*

The two *Math Skills That Work* books are designed to address the functional needs of adult students. Each book in this adult math-literacy series contains complete computation instruction and a core of functional activities interwoven for high-interest reading. The functional activities center around marketplace, workplace, and home experiences most relevant to adults. These activities are designed to pique the interest of your students and provide points for discussion, such as students' personal and classroom experiences or local newspaper ads. Special activity pages called "In Your Life" and "On the Job" highlight topics that are of particular interest and relevance to adult learners.

Each *Math Skills That Work* book can be used in independent study or in group instruction. While *Book One* covers whole numbers, money, and basic measurement topics, *Book Two* covers decimals, fractions, percents, and data analysis.

Estimation and Calculators

Another aspect of the functional approach to math is the recognition that, in today's world, most math is done either mentally or by calculator. *Math Skills That Work* responds by addressing the two math tools adults will use most often in everyday life: **estimation** and **calculators.** Throughout each book, instruction in estimation and calculator use is integrated into computation problems and functional activities. Additional activities are provided to help students learn when estimation is a reasonable alternative to computing an exact answer.

It is noteworthy that estimation is especially important when students use calculators. For example, an estimate of the quotient $588 \div 21$ is $600 \div 20 = \$30$. The estimate $30 tells students whether they pressed the correct calculator keys when dividing. A calculator answer of $28 would be reasonable (and correct) while a calculator answer of $280 would alert students to keying errors.

The *Math Skills That Work* series is designed so that you, the instructor, can emphasize computation, estimation, and calculator use at your own level of comfort and at each student's level of ability. Whenever possible, it is recommended that each student learn all three of these important skills. Ideally, students can practice estimation and calculator skills in designated exercises and get additional practice by using these tools to check answers to selected computation problems.

To the Student

Welcome to *Math Skills That Work, Book One*

This book is designed to provide you with basic math skills you can use. You'll learn to add, subtract, multiply, and divide whole numbers and money amounts. You'll also learn to apply these skills where you're most likely to need them: at home, on the job, and when shopping.

Each unit of this book has a number of features designed to make your study more enjoyable. Among these features are:

- short activities based on home, consumer, and workplace situations

- "In Your Life" activities that highlight topics of interest to consumers

- "On the Job" activities that highlight topics of interest to workers

- "Focus on Calculators" activities teach you how to use a calculator to compute the answers to a wide variety of problems

In addition, *Math Skills That Work* contains:

- special activities designed to teach you how and when to estimate instead of finding an exact answer

- unit Skill Reviews that recap the skills taught in each unit

- a comprehensive Post-Test that gives you a chance to test your mastery of many of the skills taught in this book

On a number of pages, a row of Skill Builders comes before the practice exercises. Skill Builders are problems that have been started for you. Look at the steps that have been done, then complete each problem.

To get the most out of your work, do each problem and activity carefully. Check your answers to make sure you are computing accurately. A complete answer key starts on page 185.

Becoming Familiar with Numbers

Things to do today:
- order shelves for laundry room Discount Catalog #89A-457
- make dentist appointments for kids 10/13 or 11/6
- try new dry cleaner at 1120 Lowell Street
- make brownies for church supper

Sondra may enroll in a class like this one.

"For the last time, Bill—I don't *need* to learn math. I'm a wife and a mother—what do I need with numbers?"

Sondra's husband had been trying to get her to take a class or two at the community college. When a new class in math was advertised, he urged her to check it out. He knew that Sondra would do well in it—she had a real commonsense understanding of a lot of things, including math.

Bill thought that if Sondra could see how well she worked with numbers in her everyday life, she might gain the confidence to take that math class. That could lead to a part-time office job with the school district.

"OK, Sondra," said Bill. "Look at your list of things to do today. Do you need to work with numbers to do any of these things?"

Sondra slowly read down her list. "Well, I guess I do. I have to read numbers out loud on the phone whenever I order something from a catalog. I also always check to make sure they are billing me the correct amount of money. And I have no idea where that new dry cleaner is, so I'll have to go by the numbers in the address to find it."

"And obviously you knew how to write dates using numbers—10/13. And how will you know how many brownies to make for the church supper?"

"Well, I estimate the number of people who attend each year and figure two brownies per person. From those numbers I can easily adapt whatever recipe I'm working with. I really do use a lot of numbers! Let me see that math class schedule, will you?"

Think About It

- Imagine that you are Sondra. Jot down some other situations in which she might use numbers in her daily activities.

How Do Numbers Play a Part in *Your* Life?

Like Sondra, you may not even be aware of how often you use numbers every day. In fact, you may be so sure that you don't know anything about numbers that the whole idea of math makes you uneasy. In this unit and throughout this book, however, you will be able to concentrate on ways in which you already use numbers successfully. You will also learn new ways to use numbers.

To get to know how numbers play a part in your life, answer the following questions:

Describe two recent occasions when you had to write down a number.

1) _____

2) _____

Describe two occasions when you had to read or say a number out loud.

1) _____

2) _____

When was the last time you used a street address to find a place you had never been to before? What made the task difficult? What made it easy?

_____

_____

Name two times when you compared numbers. Were you looking for the largest number or the smallest number? Why?

_____

_____

Skills You Will Learn

Number Skills
- reading numbers
- writing numbers
- writing dollars and cents

Life and Workplace Skills
- writing checks
- filing by numbers
- using addresses
- writing and using dates

Thinking Skills
- comparing numbers
- rounding numbers
- rounding dollars and cents

Calculator Skills
- using calculator keys
- displaying numbers

Familiar Numbers

Numbers are formed by writing one or more of the ten **digits** of our number system. Each digit represents a group of objects.

```
□  □□  □□  □□  □□  □□  □□  □□  □□  □□
0   1   2   3   4   5   6   7   8   9
```

A two-digit number is written by placing two digits next to each other. The order in which the digits are written determines the value of the number.

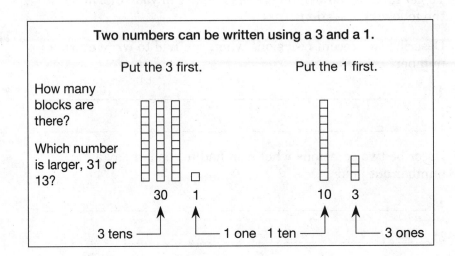

Place Value

Two-digit numbers tell how many groups of ten and how many ones there are:
- the digit on the left is in the **tens place**
- the digit on the right is in the **ones place**

$$\underset{\text{tens place}}{3} \quad \underset{\text{ones place}}{1}$$

Two numbers can be written using a 3 and a 1.

Put the 3 first.   Put the 1 first.

How many blocks are there?

Which number is larger, 31 or 13?

30   1   10   3

3 tens —— 1 one   1 ten —— 3 ones

The First Four Place Values

Most numbers you'll ever use will have four or fewer digits. The number 1,326 is an example of a four-digit number. The **value** of each digit is determined by its **place** in the number.

$$\underset{1{,}000\text{s}}{1}, \ \underset{100\text{s}}{3} \ \underset{10\text{s}}{2} \ \underset{1\text{s}}{6}$$

1 thousand ——→   6 ones
3 hundreds ——→   2 tens

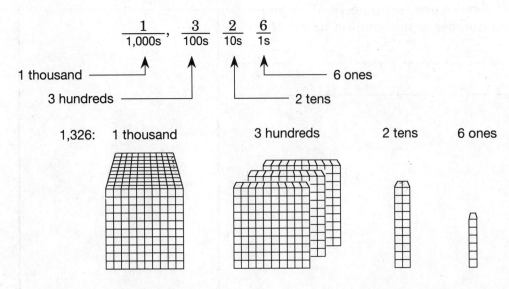

1,326:   1 thousand   3 hundreds   2 tens   6 ones

Writing Zero as a Place Holder

Zero is often used as a **place holder**.

- Zero can be used to show that there are no hundreds, no tens, or no ones.

When writing numbers, place a comma between the thousands and the hundreds digits.

Examples:

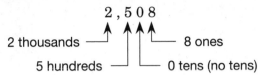

2 thousands ⟶
5 hundreds ⟶
8 ones
0 tens (no tens)

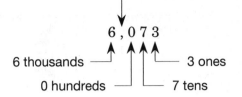

6 thousands ⟶
0 hundreds ⟶
3 ones
7 tens

▼ Practice

How many blocks are in each drawing below?

1. _____

2. _____

3. _____

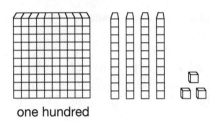

one hundred

4. _____

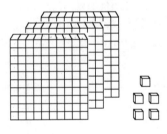

5. _____

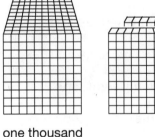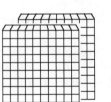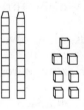

one thousand

How many of each?

6. 17 has _____ ten and _____ ones.

7. 49 has _____ tens and _____ ones.

8. 150 has _____ hundred, _____ tens, and _____ ones.

9. 748 has _____ hundreds, _____ tens, and _____ ones.

10. 1,538 has _____ thousand, _____ hundreds, _____ tens, and _____ ones.

11. 4,095 has _____ thousands, _____ hundreds, _____ tens, and _____ ones.

12. 8,640 has _____ thousands, _____ hundreds, _____ tens, and _____ ones.

Writing Whole Numbers

Take time now to make sure you can spell each number below.

You may need to write out a number when you write a check or fill out a form.

Number	Word	Number	Word	Number	Word
0	zero	10	ten	20	twenty
1	one	11	eleven	30	thirty
2	two	12	twelve	40	forty
3	three	13	thirteen	50	fifty
4	four	14	fourteen	60	sixty
5	five	15	fifteen	70	seventy
6	six	16	sixteen	80	eighty
7	seven	17	seventeen	90	ninety
8	eight	18	eighteen	100	one hundred
9	nine	19	nineteen	1,000	one thousand

▼ Practice

A. Carla takes catalog orders over the phone. She must correctly write down order numbers that she hears. Complete the order form at right. The first one is done for you.

Phoned-In Catalog Order Numbers

1. "A, eight, three, zero, dash, two, four, five"

2. "A, nine, seven, zero, dash, one, six, eight"

3. "B, zero, zero, five, dash, four, eight, one"

4. "C, six, two, four, dash, nine, seven, eight"

Catalog Order Form

1. A830-245
2. _____
3. _____
4. _____

B. George's boss asked him to write each amount in words on the wholesale price list. Complete the price list below.

Item	Price		Item	Price	
1.	$17 _seventeen_	dollars	6.	$90 _____	dollars
2.	$14 _____	dollars	7.	$300 _____	dollars
3.	$12 _____	dollars	8.	$400 _____	dollars
4.	$40 _____	dollars	9.	$7,000 _____	dollars
5.	$50 _____	dollars	10.	$9,000 _____	dollars

Look at these next three examples:

47 is written forty-seven.

65 is written sixty-five.

Place a hyphen (-) in numbers between twenty-one (21) and ninety-nine (99).

2,435 is written two thousand, four hundred thirty-five.

The word *and* is not used when writing or saying whole numbers.

Place a comma after the word *thousand* but not after the word *hundred*.

C. Shauna was quoted the following prices over the phone. Write each price in numbers on the purchase order form at right.

1. "The drop spreader is thirty-eight dollars."

2. "Ten sacks of fertilizer are forty-six dollars."

3. "The power mower costs two hundred fifteen dollars."

4. "The chain saw is three hundred eighty-nine dollars."

5. "The riding mower is one thousand, eight hundred seventy-two dollars."

PURCHASE ORDER	
Item	**Total Price**
1. Spreader	$ _____38_____
2. Fertilizer	$ _____
3. Power Mower	$ _____
4. Chain Saw	$ _____
5. Riding Mower	$ _____

D. Write each number below in words.

1. 21 _____

2. 48 _____

3. 192 _____

4. 305 _____three hundred five_____

5. 6,000 _____

6. 5,090 ___five thousand, ninety___

7. 7,840 _____

8. 35 _____thirty-five_____

9. 72 _____

10. 256 _____

11. 802 _____

12. 9,000 _____

13. 4,040 _____

14. 9,360 _____

Writing Dollars and Cents

The most commonly used United States coins and bills are shown below.

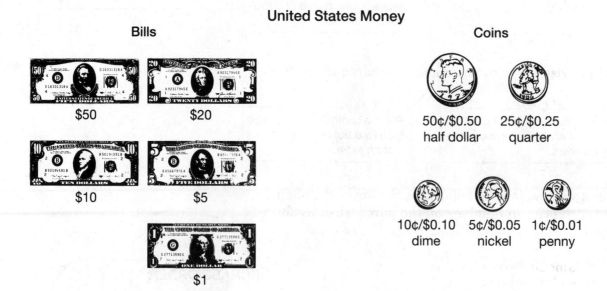

United States Money

Bills

$50 $20

$10 $5

$1

Coins

50¢/$0.50   25¢/$0.25
half dollar   quarter

10¢/$0.10   5¢/$0.05   1¢/$0.01
dime   nickel   penny

To combine dollars and cents, we use a **dollar sign** and **decimal point**.

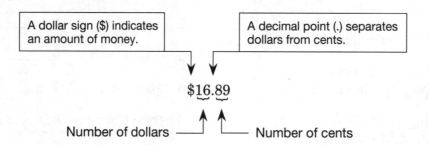

A dollar sign ($) indicates an amount of money.

A decimal point (.) separates dollars from cents.

$16.89

Number of dollars ——— Number of cents

- When reading or writing dollars and cents, treat the decimal point as the word *and*.

  $16.89 is read "16 dollars *and* 89 cents."

- For cents between 1¢ and 9¢, write a zero between the decimal point and the cents digit.

  5 dollars and 8 cents is written $5.08.

- Cents can be written with or without a zero in the dollar column.

  16 cents is written $0.16 or $.16.

- A dollar amount with no cents can be written two ways.

  $17 is the same amount as $17.00.

Write each amount below using a dollar sign and decimal point.

1. Seven dollars and nine cents ___$7.09___

2. Twenty-three dollars and six cents _____

3. Forty-one dollars and eight cents _____

4. Seventy-two dollars and twenty-five cents _____

5. One hundred twelve dollars and ninety cents _____

6. Two hundred four dollars and sixty-one cents _____

7. Five hundred fifty dollars and thirty cents _____

8. Nine hundred dollars and two cents _____

Write each amount below. On the first line, use the cents sign. On the second line, use the dollar sign and decimal point.

9. five cents ___5¢___ ___$.05 or $0.05___

10. eight cents _____ _____

11. two cents _____ _____

12. seven cents _____ _____

13. forty-six cents _____ _____

14. eighty-three cents _____ _____

15. seventy-nine cents _____ _____

16. twenty-one cents _____ _____

Write each amount below in words.

17. $6.09 ___six dollars and nine cents___

18. $8.92 _____

19. $14.05 _____

20. $74.53 _____

21. $156.78 _____

22. $357.40 _____

23. $1,032.50 _____

24. $1,506.90 _____

Writing a Check

Do you write checks at home or work? To write a check, you write the amount of money both in numbers and in words. The check below is completed as an example.

Write today's date.

Write the person or company you are paying.

Write the amount in numbers.

Write the dollar amount in words. Write the cents as shown.

Sign your name.

287
May 7 19 X   31-20
427

PAY TO THE
ORDER OF *Corner Market* $ *12.85*

Twelve and 85/100 ——————— DOLLARS

HOME
BANK   Downtown Branch
Chicago, Illinois

MEMO _____
67 - 004--459   00-746

Bill Lewis

▼ Practice

Fill in each check using the information to the left of the check.

Check 288

To: The Book Den
For: $7.95
Today's date
Your signature

288
_____19___   31-20
427

PAY TO THE
ORDER OF_____ $ _____

_____ DOLLARS

HOME
BANK   Downtown Branch
Chicago, Illinois

MEMO_____   _____
67 - 004--459   00-746

Check 289

To: Ben's Market
For: $23.46
Today's date
Your signature

289
_____19___   31-20
427

PAY TO THE
ORDER OF_____ $ _____

_____ DOLLARS

HOME
BANK   Downtown Branch
Chicago, Illinois

MEMO_____   _____
67 - 004--459   00-746

Check 290

To: Crest Apartments
For: $295.50
Today's date
Your signature

	290
_____ 19___	$\frac{31\text{-}20}{427}$

PAY TO THE
ORDER OF_____ $ _____

_____ DOLLARS

⌂ **HOME
BANK** Downtown Branch
Chicago, Illinois

MEMO_____ _____
67 - 004--459   00-746

Check 291

To: Yogurt Plus
For: $10.00
Today's date
Your signature

(Hint: Write 00 cents as no/100)

	291
_____ 19___	$\frac{31\text{-}20}{427}$

PAY TO THE
ORDER OF_____ $ _____

_____ DOLLARS

⌂ **HOME
BANK** Downtown Branch
Chicago, Illinois

MEMO_____ _____
67 - 004--459   00-746

Check 292

To: Value Shopping
For: $17.82
Today's date
Your signature

	292
_____ 19___	$\frac{31\text{-}20}{427}$

PAY TO THE
ORDER OF_____ $ _____

_____ DOLLARS

⌂ **HOME
BANK** Downtown Branch
Chicago, Illinois

MEMO_____ _____
67 - 004--459   00-746

Check 293

To: City Parks Program
For: $27.00
Today's date
Your signature

	293
_____ 19___	$\frac{31\text{-}20}{427}$

PAY TO THE
ORDER OF_____ $ _____

_____ DOLLARS

⌂ **HOME
BANK** Downtown Branch
Chicago, Illinois

MEMO_____ _____
67 - 004--459   00-746

Comparing Numbers

Comparing numbers is a skill that you may use daily, often without even thinking about it!

To compare numbers, remember these points:

- When two whole numbers have a different number of digits, the whole number with more digits is larger.

Which is heavier?

965 lb. or 1,035 lb.

Answer: 1,035 lb.
Reason: 1,035 has 4 digits.
965 has 3 digits.

- When two whole numbers have the same number of digits, compare digits from left to right.

Which town is closer to Canby?

Canby   473 miles   Owen
458 miles   Harper

Answer: Harper (458 miles)
Reason: Seeing that both numbers start with 4, you compare the next digit: 45**8** miles is closer than 47**3** miles.

- When comparing money amounts, compare the number of dollars first.

Which costs less?

 $17.46 or $16.99

Answer: $16.99
Reason: 16 is smaller than 17.

▼ Practice

Write A, B, or C to show in which building each room can be found.

Example: Room 145 is found in Building A because 145 is larger than 101 but smaller than 177—the lowest number in Building B.

Building A
101–176

Building B	Building C
177–252	253–308

1. Room 182 ____   Room 117 ____   Room 282 ____

2. Room 301 ____   Room 212 ____   Room 163 ____

List the checks in order of check number.
List the lowest number check first, and so on.
One is listed as an example.

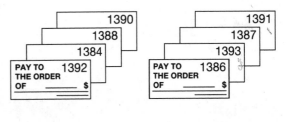

3. _____ _____ 1387 _____
   (1st) (2nd) (3rd) (4th)

   _____ _____ _____ _____
   (5th) (6th) (7th) (8th)

Circle the best buy in each group below.

4.

$0.48 $0.39 $0.42
per lb.   per lb.   per lb.

6.

$8.92 $10.19 $9.48

5.

$1.83 $1.79 $1.76

7.

$13.79 $14.09 $15.75

8. Record the following payments in the Payment Book below.

Customer	Payment
Amy Smythe	$143.65
Billy Adamly	96.00
Emma James	225.00
Greg Phillips	45.75
Harold Lerronde	28.50

Payment Book					
Customer:	Adamly	James	Lerronde	Phillips	Smythe
Amount Owed:	$243.81	$175.00	$113.45	$45.75	$343.00
Payment:	_____	_____	_____	_____	_____

9. Which customer made: the largest payment? _____

   the smallest payment? _____

10. Which customer paid the exact balance of his or her bill? _____

11. Which customer overpaid and should receive a refund? _____

Filing in Numerical Order

To **file** a document is to place it in order in a document holder such as a file drawer.

- Filing by letter is called **alphabetical filing**.
  Example: Filing patients' files in a doctor's office.

- Filing by an identifying number is called **numerical filing**.
  Example: Filing company billing forms (invoices).

> To file numerically, you place a document so that its file number falls between the file numbers of two already-filed documents.

Example: In which location (A, B, or C) should each document below be filed?

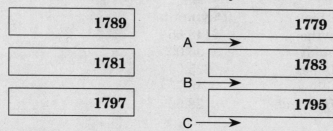

Documents to be filed	Already filed documents
1789	1779
1781	1783
1797	1795

- Document 1789 should be filed at B.
  1789 is larger than 1783 but smaller than 1795.

- Document 1781 should be filed at A.
  1781 is larger than 1779 but smaller than 1783.

- Document 1797 should be filed at C.
  1797 is larger than 1795.

▼ Practice

File each folder below in the file drawer at right. Write A, B, or C to the left of each folder to show in which section of the drawer the folder belongs.

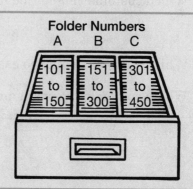

Folder Numbers
A   B   C

101 to 150   151 to 300   301 to 450

1. __B__ | 163
2. ____ | 142
3. ____ | 412
4. ____ | 239
5. ____ | 317
6. ____ | 108

File each folder in the correct file drawer. Write the number
of the folder on the line to the left of the correct drawer.
(More than 1 folder may go into each drawer.)

Folders

1768

1721

1802

1711

1765

1834

1719

File Drawers

7. _____ Folder Numbers
1681 to 1718

8. _____ Folder Numbers
1719 to 1761

9. _____ Folder Numbers
1762 to 1796

10. _____ Folder Numbers
1797 to 1834

11. _____ Folder Numbers
1835 to 1879

Look at the billing information listed on the computer
screen below, and then answer the questions that follow.

INVOICE #	BALANCE DUE	COMPANY
C147	$4,462.75	Adex, Inc.
C148	$3,205.25	Johnson's
C150	$7,500.00	Hillside
C151	$1,850.00	Medical, Inc.
C152	$3,217.48	Electro Plus
C154	$1,685.50	Corl Bros.

12. Which two invoice numbers are missing in the sequence
from C147 to C154?

_____   _____

13. List the billing information in the order of Balance Due.
List the largest balance first, and so on.

Balance Due	Invoice #		Balance Due	Invoice #
1st: _____	_____	4th:	_____	_____
2nd: _____	_____	5th:	_____	_____
3rd: _____	_____	6th:	_____	_____

IN YOUR LIFE

Understanding Addresses

An address tells the location of a house or other building.

Most addresses follow the pattern described below.

Block numbers are written to the left of the tens place. Block numbers may tell how far a block is from a street running through the center of town.

Block Number

1 3 4 8 Oak Street

Building Number

Buildings are numbered by tens and ones.

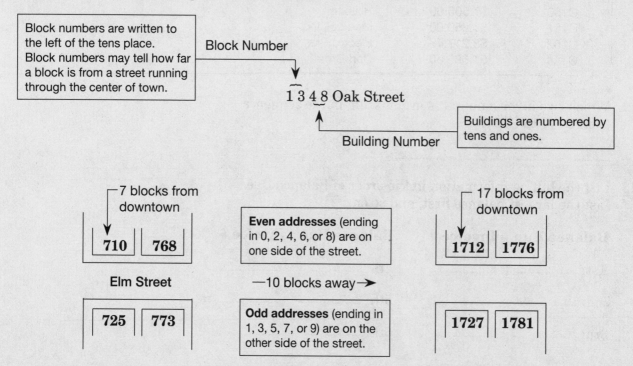

7 blocks from downtown

| 710 | 768 |

Even addresses (ending in 0, 2, 4, 6, or 8) are on one side of the street.

17 blocks from downtown

| 1712 | 1776 |

Elm Street

—10 blocks away→

| 725 | 773 |

Odd addresses (ending in 1, 3, 5, 7, or 9) are on the other side of the street.

| 1727 | 1781 |

▼ Practice

Match pairs of addresses that are on the same block. Write a matching letter on the line before each address.

_____ 1. 1376 North 14th Street

_____ 2. 310 Bay View Drive

_____ 3. 310 South 14th Street

_____ 4. 3760 Bay View Drive

_____ 5. 376 North 14th Street

_____ 6. 1310 South 14th Street

a) 376 Bay View Drive

b) 310 North 14th Street

c) 1376 South 14th Street

d) 1310 North 14th Street

e) 376 South 14th Street

f) 3700 Bay View Drive

Fill in each blank below. Even-numbered addresses are on the north side of each street. The first one has been done for you.

Address	Blocks from Main Street?	Side of Street? North or South	
7. 384 Holloway Dr.	3	✔	
8. 698 Franklin St.	___	___	___
9. 1255 Highland Dr.	___	___	___
10. 410 Illinois Ave.	___	___	___
11. 3479 Rose Dr.	___	___	___
12. 4787 Kirkland Rd.	___	___	___

```
                    ┌──────────────────────┐
                    │  ┌ ─ ─ ─ ─ ─ ─ ─ ─    │
                    │  │  Holloway Dr.       │
                  ↑ │  └ ─ ─ ─ ─ ─ ─ ─ ─     │
                  N │  ┌ ─ ─ ─ ─ ─ ─ ─ ─     │
                    │  │  Franklin St.       │
              Main  │  └ ─ ─ ─ ─ ─ ─ ─ ─     │
              Street│  ┌ ─ ─ ─ ─ ─ ─ ─ ─     │
                    │  │  Highland Dr.       │
                    │  └ ─ ─ ─ ─ ─ ─ ─ ─     │
                    │  ┌ ─ ─ ─ ─ ─ ─ ─ ─     │
                    │  │  Illinois Ave.      │
                    │  └ ─ ─ ─ ─ ─ ─ ─ ─     │
                    │  ┌ ─ ─ ─ ─ ─ ─ ─ ─     │
                    │  │  Rose Dr.           │
                    │  └ ─ ─ ─ ─ ─ ─ ─ ─     │
                    │  ┌ ─ ─ ─ ─ ─ ─ ─ ─     │
                    │  │  Kirkland Rd.       │
                    │  └ ─ ─ ─ ─ ─ ─ ─ ─     │
                    └──────────────────────┘
```

13. Write an address on each building that doesn't show one now. Choose from the list of addresses at right.

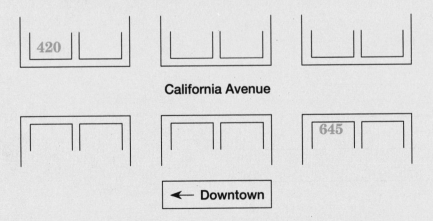

California Avenue

← Downtown

Addresses

524	597
618	499
443	698
588	494
695	541

Writing Dates as Numbers

Job application forms and business forms often ask you to write **dates** as numbers. In the United States, here's how you do it.

- First, write the number of the month.

- Second, write the number of the day of the month.

- Third, write the last two numbers of the year.

Example: Write May 29, 1944, in numbers.

Between Slashes

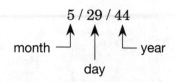

month — day — year

In Boxes

0 5   2 9   4 4

If you don't need two spaces for a month (or day), place a 0 in the extra box.

▼ Practice

Write the following dates as indicated. The first one has been done for you.

		Between Slashes	**In Boxes**
1. June 19, 1978		6 /19 /78	0 6 1 9 7 8
2. December 13, 1985		__ /__ /__	☐☐ ☐☐ ☐☐
3. April 3, 1991		__ /__ /__	☐☐ ☐☐ ☐☐
4. Your birth date		__ /__ /__	☐☐ ☐☐ ☐☐
5. Today's date		__ /__ /__	☐☐ ☐☐ ☐☐

Write out the following dates.

6. 7/9/60 _____ July 9, 1960 _____

7. 3/17/82 _____

8. 8/20/91 _____

9. 0 5 3 1 7 9 _____

10. 1 2 0 5 9 3 _____

Comparing Dates

- To compare dates, first compare years, then months, and then days.

Example: Write the following dates in the order in which they occurred.

  4/25/62   9/08/60   5/27/60

Step 1. Compare the years.

  9/08/60 and 5/27/60 are 1960 dates and occurred before 4/25/62, a 1962 date.

Step 2. Compare the months.

  5/27/60, a May date, occurred before 9/08/60, a September date.

Answer: 1st: 5/27/60   2nd: 9/08/60   3rd: 4/25/62

---

11. In each group below, list the dates in order. Place a 1 by the date that occurred first, etc.

A. ___ **a)** 6/18/90   **B.** ___ **a)** [0][4] [0][8] [9][1]

  ___ **b)** 8/03/90   ___ **b)** [1][0] [0][4] [9][0]

  ___ **c)** 3/24/90   ___ **c)** [0][5] [1][1] [9][1]

  ___ **d)** 1/30/90   ___ **d)** [0][9] [1][8] [9][0]

  ___ **e)** 12/01/90   ___ **e)** [0][3] [2][7] [9][1]

12. File each folder by date. Write the date of the folder on the line to the left of the correct file drawer.

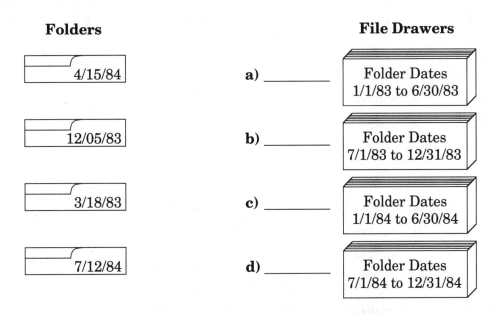

Folders

  4/15/84

  12/05/83

  3/18/83

  7/12/84

File Drawers

a) _____ | Folder Dates 1/1/83 to 6/30/83

b) _____ | Folder Dates 7/1/83 to 12/31/83

c) _____ | Folder Dates 1/1/84 to 6/30/84

d) _____ | Folder Dates 7/1/84 to 12/31/84

Understanding Larger Numbers

In larger numbers, commas separate digits in groups of three.
Notice the pattern of 100s, 10s, and 1s in each group.

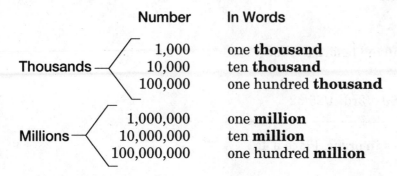

Millions	Thousands	Ones

___ ___ ___ , ___ ___ ___ , ___ ___ ___
100s 10s 1s   100s 10s 1s   100s 10s 1s

To see how place value is read in larger numbers, look at these examples:

	Number	In Words
Thousands	1,000	one **thousand**
	10,000	ten **thousand**
	100,000	one hundred **thousand**
Millions	1,000,000	one **million**
	10,000,000	ten **million**
	100,000,000	one hundred **million**

- To read a larger number, read each group of digits separately.

348, 239, 675 is read 348 *million*, 239 *thousand*, 675.

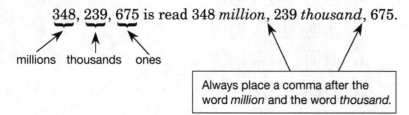

millions thousands ones

Always place a comma after the word *million* and the word *thousand*.

▼ Practice

How many of each?

1. 45,390 has __45__ thousands, __390__ ones.

2. 93,057 has _____ thousands, _____ ones.

3. 250,000 has _____ thousands, _____ ones.

4. 734,825 has _____ thousands, _____ ones.

5. 6,540,300 has __6__ millions, __540__ thousands, __300__ ones.

6. 9,450,950 has _____ millions, _____ thousands, _____ ones.

7. 45,750,000 has _____ millions, _____ thousands, _____ ones.

8. 75,125,600 has _____ millions, _____ thousands, _____ ones.

9. 245,800,000 has _____ millions, _____ thousands, _____ ones.

10. 650,985,450 has _____ millions, _____ thousands, _____ ones.

A. Match each number with the correct word expression.
Write the correct letter on the line next to the number.

Numbers	Word Expressions
_____ 1. 240,000	**a)** twenty million, four hundred thousand
_____ 2. 2,400,000	**b)** two million, four thousand
_____ 3. 24,000,000	**c)** two million, four hundred thousand
_____ 4. 204,000	**d)** two hundred forty thousand
_____ 5. 20,400,000	**e)** two hundred four thousand
_____ 6. 2,040,000	**f)** twenty-four million
_____ 7. 20,040,000	**g)** two million, forty thousand
_____ 8. 2,004,000	**h)** twenty million, forty thousand

B. Sonja's boss is dictating the following numbers.
Write each on the summary sheet as shown.

Dictated Numbers

1. nine thousand, five hundred

2. five thousand, one hundred forty

3. forty-two thousand, six hundred

4. fifty-eight thousand, nine hundred sixty

5. one hundred thirty-five thousand, seven hundred

6. three hundred ninety-four thousand, five hundred seventy

7. five million, eight hundred thousand

8. nine million, four hundred fifty thousand, three hundred

9. twenty-six million, forty-five thousand

10. two hundred eighty million, five hundred thousand

Summary Sheet
1. _____9,500_____
2. _____
3. _____
4. _____
5. _____
6. _____
7. _____
8. _____
9. _____
10. _____

C. Write the following numbers in words.

11. The largest number Juan can display on his calculator is
99,999,999. Write this number in words.

12. Sally read a report that estimated the population of the
United States to be 248,750,000. Write this number in
words.

Rounding Whole Numbers

Often, it is useful to **estimate**—to give a number that is "about equal" to an exact amount.

1 , 2 3 4 , 5 6 7

Place Values

- A sports announcer says that 500 people entered a Labor Day Jog-A-Thon. (Actually, 476 people are entered.)

The number 500 is called a **round number.** A round number has zeros on the end. 500 has zeros everywhere but the hundreds place.

- To the hundreds place, 476 rounds to 500.

Example 1: Round 35 to the nearest ten.

Ask: "Is 35 closer to 30 or to 40?"

Answer: 35 rounds to 40. A number that is halfway or more *always rounds up*—to the larger round number.

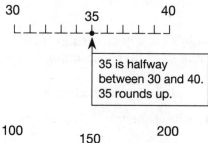

35 is halfway between 30 and 40. 35 rounds up.

Example 2: Round 143 to the nearest hundred.

Ask: "Is 143 closer to 100 or to 200?"

Answer: 143 rounds to 100. A number that is less than halfway *always rounds down*.

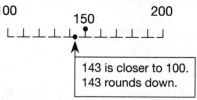

143 is closer to 100. 143 rounds down.

Example 3: Round 2,678 to the nearest thousand.

Ask: "Is 2,678 closer to 2,000 or to 3,000?"

Answer: 3,000

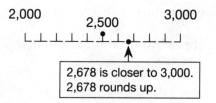

2,678 is closer to 3,000. 2,678 rounds up.

▼ **MATH TIP**   When rounding, look at the digit to the right of the place you're rounding to.

- If the digit is 5 or more, round up.
- If the digit is less than 5, round down.

Examples:

Nearest ten	Nearest hundred	Nearest thousand
48 rounds to 50	534 rounds to 500	2,481 rounds to 2,000
5 or more (round up)	less than 5 (round down)	less than 5 (round down)

▼ Practice

Circle your answer choices in problems 1–4.

To Guess	Estimate to the Nearest		
1. the number of vitamin pills left in a nearly empty bottle	10	100	1,000
2. the number of spectators in a large football stadium	10	10,000	1,000,000
3. the number of sunny days last summer	1	10	100
4. the number of school-age children in the United States	1,000	10,000	1,000,000

Round each number below as indicated. Circle each answer choice.

To the nearest ten	To the nearest hundred	To the nearest thousand
5. 67: 60 or 70	346: 300 or 400	3,680: 3,000 or 4,000
6. 35: 30 or 40	853: 800 or 900	6,850: 6,000 or 7,000
7. $53: $50 or $60	$368: $300 or $400	$2,430: $2,000 or $3,000
8. 151: 150 or 160	1,960: 1,900 or 2,000	12,490: 12,000 or 13,000

Round each number below as indicated.

	Exact Number	Estimate
9. maximum seating at Tino's Italian Restaurant	83	_____ (nearest 10)
10. Ernie's monthly salary	$1,462	_____ (nearest $100)
11. the cost of a new car	$11,436	_____ (nearest $1,000)
12. the average distance in miles of the moon from the earth	237,300	_____ (nearest 10,000)
13. the average distance in miles of the sun from the earth	92,900,000	_____ (nearest 1,000,000)

Rounding Dollars and Cents

When rounding money, you'll most often round to the nearest $1.00 or nearest $10.00.

Rounding to the Nearest Dollar
- Look at the number of cents.

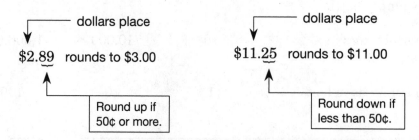

dollars place

$2.89 rounds to $3.00

Round up if 50¢ or more.

dollars place

$11.25 rounds to $11.00

Round down if less than 50¢.

Rounding to the Nearest Ten Dollars
- Look at the number of dollars.

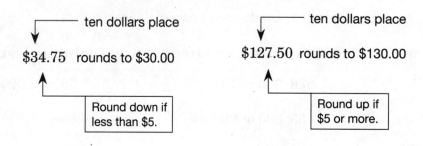

ten dollars place

$34.75 rounds to $30.00

Round down if less than $5.

ten dollars place

$127.50 rounds to $130.00

Round up if $5 or more.

▼ Practice

Round each purchase to the nearest dollar.

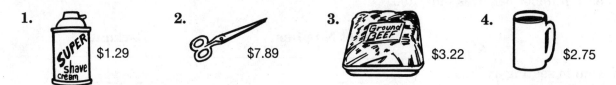

1. $1.29

2. $7.89

3. $3.22

4. $2.75

Round each purchase to the nearest ten dollars.

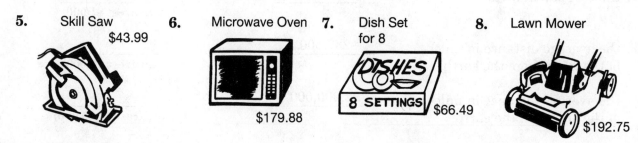

5. Skill Saw $43.99

6. Microwave Oven $179.88

7. Dish Set for 8 $66.49

8. Lawn Mower $192.75

FOCUS ON CALCULATORS

Calculators are becoming important in the study of math, both at home and on the job. In *Math Skills That Work*, you'll learn to use a calculator to solve a variety of math problems.

The Calculator Keyboard

The calculator below is probably similar to one you've seen, or one you may be using.

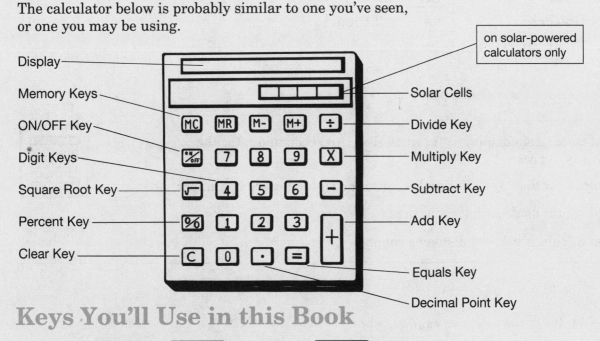

Display
Memory Keys
ON/OFF Key
Digit Keys
Square Root Key
Percent Key
Clear Key

on solar-powered calculators only

Solar Cells
Divide Key
Multiply Key
Subtract Key
Add Key
Equals Key
Decimal Point Key

Keys You'll Use in this Book

- The **on/off key** (ON/OFF). You press (ON/OFF) once to turn a calculator on, and press it again to turn the calculator off. Some calculators have separate (ON) and (OFF) keys.

- The **digit keys** (0), (1), (2), (3), (4), (5), (6), (7), (8), and (9). You press digit keys to enter a number on a calculator. Entering a number is similar to dialing on a touch-tone telephone. You simply press one digit at a time.

- The **function keys** (+), (−), (×), and (÷). You press a function key each time you add, subtract, multiply, or divide.

- The **decimal point key** $\boxed{\cdot}$. For example, in problems involving money, you press $\boxed{\cdot}$ to separate dollars from cents.

- The **equals key** $\boxed{=}$. Pressing $\boxed{=}$ completes a calculation and tells the calculator to display the answer.

- The **clear key** $\boxed{C}$. Pressing $\boxed{C}$ erases the display. You press $\boxed{C}$ each time you begin a new problem, or when you've made a keying error.

Different calculators use different clear key symbols. The most common symbols are shown below.

$\boxed{C}$	**Clear**	$\boxed{CE/C}$	**Clear Entry/Clear**
$\boxed{ON/C}$	**On/Clear**	$\boxed{AC}$	**All Clear**
$\boxed{CE}$	**Clear Entry**		

Calculator Discovery

- Most calculators display a "0." when first turned on and after the clear key is pressed.

- A calculator displays a decimal point to the right of a whole number.

- A calculator does not have a comma (,) key.

- Most calculators do not display a comma.

Displayed Numbers

Look carefully at the next two examples.

Example 1: To enter 4,630 on your calculator, press keys as shown at right.

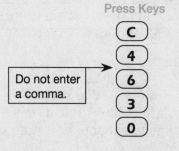

Press Keys	Display Reads
$\boxed{C}$	
$\boxed{4}$	4.
$\boxed{6}$	4 6.
$\boxed{3}$	4 6 3.
$\boxed{0}$	4 6 3 0.

Do not enter a comma.

Example 2: To enter $5.83 on your calculator, press keys as shown at right.

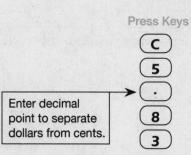

Press Keys	Display Reads
$\boxed{C}$	0.
$\boxed{5}$	5.
$\boxed{\cdot}$	5.
$\boxed{8}$	5 . 8
$\boxed{3}$	5 . 8 3

Enter decimal point to separate dollars from cents.

Use your calculator to answer the following questions.

1. Is your calculator solar powered or battery powered?

_____

2. Which key do you press to turn your calculator on?
(Some solar-powered calculators do not have an On or Off
key—only a cover that opens and closes!)

_____

3. When turned on, what does your calculator display?

_____

4. With your calculator on, press the whole number keys in
order:

(1), (2), (3), (4), (5), (6), (7), (8), (9)

_____

a) How many digits appear on the display?
(Most calculators show 6 or 8.)

_____

b) What is the largest number that your calculator can
display?

_____

5. Which key do you press to clear your calculator's display? _____

6. What appears on the display after you push the clear key? _____

7. Enter the following numbers or amounts on your
calculator. Then show how the calculator displays each
entry.

Enter	Display Reads
a) 27	2 7.
b) 540	
c) 4,895	
d) $6.98	
e) $.75	

8. Which key do you press to turn your calculator off? _____

9. Does your calculator have these other keys?

a) memory keys   (MC) (MR) (M−) (M+)   yes or no

b) percent key   (%)   yes or no

c) square root key (√)   yes or no

Addition

Tony is a night clerk at the local convenience store. The manager, Ms. Greene, is giving him some instructions before she leaves for the night.

Inventory control is an important part of store management.

Ms. Greene: Don't forget to finish the dairy product inventory before you close up for the night.

Tony: OK. First I'll count up the milk, cheese, ice cream, and yogurt in the storeroom. Then I'll add those amounts to the numbers you recorded already on the inventory sheet.

Ms. Greene: Right. Be sure to do it carefully. I use that inventory to reorder, and I can't overstock the dairy products.

Tony: Why not?

Ms. Greene: Because after 10 days in the store, dairy products start to spoil. We'd end up throwing away a lot of things that we paid for. Speaking of money, have you been having any trouble with that old cash register? I think I may need to get it fixed.

Tony: Hey, I'm glad you mentioned that. Last night I almost charged a customer $21.70 for a gallon of milk and a candy bar! I estimated the total cost to be about $3.00 and realized that the cash register total didn't make sense. So I did the adding by hand and came up with $2.17, not $21.70.

Ms. Greene: Nice work. Here, take my calculator and use it with tonight's customers. You can use it to check your inventory totals, too. See you tomorrow!

Think About It

• Jot down all the things Tony and Ms. Greene discussed that involved addition.

• How many different ways of adding did they talk about?

How Does Addition Play a Part in *Your* Life?

Adding numbers. When do you do it? Why? When is adding hard? When is it easy? How do you add? Do you use paper and pen? Do you use a calculator? Do you add in your head?

In this unit, you'll learn about ways to add numbers for different situations. But before you go on, take some time now to learn about the ways in which addition plays a part in your life.

Name two situations at work in which you had to add numbers together:

1) _____

2) _____

Describe two times in the past week when you added amounts of money together:

1) _____

2) _____

Describe an occasion where adding numbers was difficult for you. What kind of numbers were you adding?

1) _____

2) _____

Have you ever estimated to get a "rough idea" of what two numbers added up to? Why didn't you need an exact answer?

_____

_____

Skills You Will Learn

Number Skills
- simple adding
- adding and carrying
- adding dollars and cents

Life and Workplace Skills
- reading a table
- counting calories
- adding coins
- working with a sales bill
- completing a catalog order form

Thinking Skills
- choosing necessary information
- estimating

Calculator Skills
- adding whole numbers
- adding dollars and cents

Adding Single Digits

To **add** is to combine or to put together.
As shown in the example, the **plus sign** (+) indicates addition.

Example:

$$\underset{\textbf{pennies}}{\underline{\hspace{1cm}5\hspace{1cm}}} \quad + \quad \underset{\textbf{pennies}}{\underline{\hspace{1cm}3\hspace{1cm}}} \quad = \quad \underset{\textbf{pennies in all}}{\underline{\hspace{1cm}8\hspace{1cm}}} \quad \text{or} \quad \begin{array}{r} 5 \text{ pennies} \\ + \ 3 \text{ pennies} \\ \hline 8 \text{ pennies} \end{array}$$

↑
Sum
(the answer)

> When two groups of objects are added, a single, larger group—called the **sum**—is formed.

▼ Practice

Write numbers for the following additions.

1.

$$\underset{\textbf{stamps}}{\underline{\hspace{2cm}}} \quad + \quad \underset{\textbf{stamps}}{\underline{\hspace{2cm}}} \quad = \quad \underset{\textbf{stamps in all}}{\underline{\hspace{2cm}}} \quad \text{or} \quad \begin{array}{r} \underline{\hspace{0.6cm}} \text{ stamps} \\ + \underline{\hspace{0.6cm}} \text{ stamps} \\ \hline \underline{\hspace{0.6cm}} \text{ stamps} \end{array}$$

2.

$$\underset{\textbf{nails}}{\underline{\hspace{2cm}}} \quad + \quad \underset{\textbf{nails}}{\underline{\hspace{2cm}}} \quad = \quad \underset{\textbf{nails altogether}}{\underline{\hspace{2cm}}} \quad \text{or} \quad \begin{array}{r} \underline{\hspace{0.6cm}} \text{ nails} \\ + \underline{\hspace{0.6cm}} \text{ nails} \\ \hline \underline{\hspace{0.6cm}} \text{ nails} \end{array}$$

3.

$$\underset{\textbf{dollars}}{\underline{\hspace{2cm}}} \quad + \quad \underset{\textbf{dollars}}{\underline{\hspace{2cm}}} \quad = \quad \underset{\textbf{total dollars}}{\underline{\hspace{2cm}}} \quad \text{or} \quad \begin{array}{r} \underline{\hspace{0.6cm}} \text{ dollars} \\ + \underline{\hspace{0.6cm}} \text{ dollars} \\ \hline \underline{\hspace{0.6cm}} \text{ dollars} \end{array}$$

Find these sums that are less than 10.

4.
4	8	2¢	6	9	4¢
+ 2	+ 1	+ 5¢	+ 3	+ 0	+ 4¢

5.
3	$5	6	1	4¢	5
+ 1	+ 3	+ 2	+ 5	+ 3¢	+ 4

6. 1 + 6 =   7 + 0 =   7 + 2 = $2 + $3 =

Find these larger sums.

7.
8	9	$5	8	2	6
+ 7	+ 4	+ 5	+ 3	+ 9	+ 6

8.
9¢	6	7	9	8	3
+ 6¢	+ 8	+ 5	+ 5	+ 8	+ 7

9. 7 + 7 =   9 + 8 =   6 + 9 = $8 + $7 =

10. 9 + 9 =   7 + 9 = $8 + $5 =   7 + 6 =

Many popular board games use dice.

What is the sum of points shown on each pair of dice below?

11. _____   12. _____   13. _____   14. _____

▼ MATH TIP

Adding digits two at a time is the way you do all addition—even when adding very large numbers.

▼ MATH TIP

When adding dollar amounts in columns, place a dollar sign on the top amount and answer only.

15. In A and B, match a sum in the second column with an
    equal sum in the first column.

A. Sums Smaller Than 10		**B.** Larger Sums	
<u>h</u> **1.** 3 + 1 **a)** 1 + 1		<u>e</u> **1.** 9 + 8 **a)** 8 + 6	
___ **2.** 7 + 2 **b)** 3 + 3		___ **2.** 8 + 7 **b)** 9 + 4	
___ **3.** 5 + 3 **c)** 0 + 3		___ **3.** 2 + 8 **c)** 6 + 9	
___ **4.** 3 + 4 **d)** 5 + 2		___ **4.** 7 + 6 **d)** 4 + 8	
___ **5.** 2 + 4 **e)** 4 + 1		___ **5.** 7 + 5 **e)** 8 + 9	
___ **6.** 2 + 0 **f)** 5 + 4		___ **6.** 9 + 7 **f)** 6 + 5	
___ **7.** 3 + 2 **g)** 6 + 2		___ **7.** 4 + 7 **g)** 7 + 3	
___ **8.** 1 + 2 **h)** 2 + 2		___ **8.** 5 + 9 **h)** 8 + 8	

Three Quick-Adding Tips

• Adding 10

To add 10 to a single digit, place a 1 in the tens place next
to the digit.

16. $10 + 8 = 18$ $10 + 9 =$ $10 + 7 =$ $5 + 10 =$

• Adding 9

To add 9, think: "The answer is one less than adding 10!"

17. $9 + 7 = 16$ $9 + 8 =$ $9 + 6 =$ $9 + 4 =$
       (one less
        than 17)

18. $8 + 9 =$ $7 + 9 =$ $5 + 9 =$ $6 + 9 =$

• Spotting Sums of 10

To simplify adding 3 or more digits, learn to quickly spot
sums that add to 10.

In each group of digits, circle two whose sum is 10.

19. ④, 7, ⑥, 5   5, 9, 3, 7   2, 4, 7, 8   1, 2, 3, 9

20. 3, 5, 8, 5   6, 3, 8, 2   7, 9, 2, 3   6, 5, 7, 4

Adding Three or More Digits

To add three or more digits:

- First, add a pair of digits.
- Then, add this sum to the next digit.

▼ MATH TIP

First look for pairs that add to 10. This makes adding easier.

Example 1:

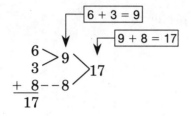

$6 + 3 = 9$

$9 + 8 = 17$

$$
\begin{array}{r}
6 \\
3 \\
+\ 8 \\
\hline
17
\end{array}
$$

Answer: 17

Example 2:

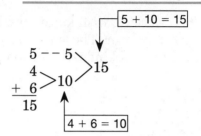

$5 + 10 = 15$

$4 + 6 = 10$

$$
\begin{array}{r}
5 \\
4 \\
+\ 6 \\
\hline
15
\end{array}
$$

Answer: 15

▼ Practice

Add. Begin by completing the partially worked Skill Builders.

Skill Builders

1.

$$
\begin{array}{r}
6 \\
3 \\
+\ 5
\end{array} \quad 9
\qquad
\begin{array}{r}
7 \\
2 \\
+\ 3
\end{array} \quad 10
\qquad
\begin{array}{r}
8 \\
0 \\
+\ 9
\end{array} \quad 8
\qquad
\begin{array}{r}
5 \\
6 \\
+\ 9
\end{array} \quad 11
\qquad
\begin{array}{r}
6 \\
7 \\
+\ 4
\end{array} \quad 10
\qquad
\begin{array}{r}
9 \\
1 \\
+\ 8
\end{array} \quad 10
$$

2.

$$
\begin{array}{r}
8 \\
8 \\
+\ 8 \\
\hline
\end{array}
\qquad
\begin{array}{r}
6¢ \\
4¢ \\
+\ 9¢ \\
\hline
\end{array}
\qquad
\begin{array}{r}
4 \\
3 \\
+\ 8 \\
\hline
\end{array}
\qquad
\begin{array}{r}
8 \\
6 \\
+\ 7 \\
\hline
\end{array}
\qquad
\begin{array}{r}
\$6 \\
5 \\
+\ 4 \\
\hline
\end{array}
\qquad
\begin{array}{r}
2 \\
8 \\
+\ 9 \\
\hline
\end{array}
$$

3.

$$
\begin{array}{r}
5¢ \\
5¢ \\
+\ 7¢ \\
\hline
\end{array}
\qquad
\begin{array}{r}
9 \\
8 \\
+\ 7 \\
\hline
\end{array}
\qquad
\begin{array}{r}
0 \\
3 \\
+\ 9 \\
\hline
\end{array}
\qquad
\begin{array}{r}
9 \\
9 \\
+\ 9 \\
\hline
\end{array}
\qquad
\begin{array}{r}
7 \\
8 \\
+\ 5 \\
\hline
\end{array}
\qquad
\begin{array}{r}
\$2 \\
9 \\
+\ 8 \\
\hline
\end{array}
$$

4.

$$
\begin{array}{r}
7 \\
6 \\
+\ 6 \\
\hline
\end{array}
\qquad
\begin{array}{r}
7 \\
9 \\
+\ 1 \\
\hline
\end{array}
\qquad
\begin{array}{r}
6¢ \\
8¢ \\
+\ 2¢ \\
\hline
\end{array}
\qquad
\begin{array}{r}
3 \\
4 \\
+\ 6 \\
\hline
\end{array}
\qquad
\begin{array}{r}
5 \\
5 \\
+\ 5 \\
\hline
\end{array}
\qquad
\begin{array}{r}
8 \\
7 \\
+\ 2 \\
\hline
\end{array}
$$

5. How much for all three? _____

$6 $5 $9

6. What is the total cost? _____

$8 $4 $2 $7

FOCUS ON CALCULATORS

Calculator Addition

When working with larger numbers, many people prefer to use a calculator. These two pages show how a calculator is used for all kinds of addition problems.

Adding Two Numbers

- The **add key** $\boxed{+}$ is used to add two numbers.
- The **equals key** $\boxed{=}$ tells the calculator to display the answer.

Remember: Press $\boxed{C}$ to clear your calculator's display before starting each new problem.

Example 1: To add 43 and 35 on your calculator, press keys as shown at right.

Press Keys	Display Reads
C	0.
4 3	4 3.
+	4 3.
3 5	3 5.
=	7 8.

Answer: 78

Adding Three or More Numbers

To add three or more numbers:

- Enter each number, and then press $\boxed{+}$.
- Press $\boxed{=}$ only after entering the final number.

Example 2: Add $3.24
             2.13
           + 1.02

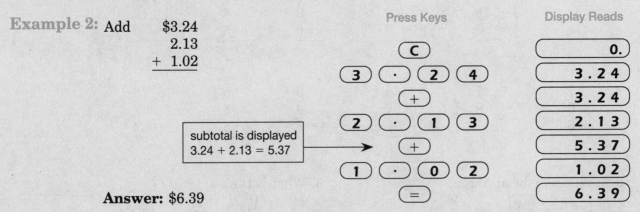

Press Keys	Display Reads
C	0.
3 . 2 4	3.24
+	3.24
2 . 1 3	2.13
+	5.37
1 . 0 2	1.02
=	6.39

subtotal is displayed
3.24 + 2.13 = 5.37

Answer: $6.39

Calculator Discovery

- The calculator display does not show a + sign.

- A final answer appears only after you press ⊜ .

- Most calculators display a **subtotal** each time you press ⊕ . A subtotal is the total sum up to the point where the ⊕ key is pressed. Does your calculator display a subtotal? (To find out, try Example 2 on page 32.)

▼ Practice

A. Fill in the key symbols to show how to calculate each answer.

Example: 23 + 14   ⓒ ② ③ ⊕ ① ④ ⊜

1. 47 + 39   ◯ ◯ ◯ ◯ ◯ ◯

2. $4.17 + $2.15   ◯ ◯ ◯ ◯ ◯ ◯ ◯ ◯ ◯ ◯

3. 2,645 + 1,350   ◯ ◯ ◯ ◯ ◯ ◯ ◯ ◯ ◯ ◯

4. 59 + 42 + 36   ◯ ◯ ◯ ◯ ◯ ◯ ◯ ◯ ◯ ◯

B. Solve these problems with your calculator.

1.
37	156	384	$1,409	$5.48
+ 21	+ 23	+ 243	+ 987	+ 4.89

2.
41	172	383	$1,850	$9.68
32	85	254	947	7.49
+ 19	+ 67	+132	+ 736	+ 5.75

3. Jeri uses her calculator to add end-of-the-month bills. How much are Jeri's monthly totals for the three months shown below?

	March	April	May
Rent	$345.75	$345.75	$345.75
Gas	174.80	152.48	147.92
Electricity	64.55	57.40	52.33
Water	27.90	32.45	34.68
Credit Card	247.85	197.00	157.41
Car Payment	147.75	147.75	147.75
Newspaper	9.60	9.60	9.60
Total:			

▼ **MATH TIP**

When adding a list of numbers, you may make a mistake on one entry. If you do, clear the display to erase this single number. Then, reenter the number correctly, and continue adding. In this way, **you do not need to redo the whole problem.**

Adding Larger Numbers

When adding larger numbers, start with the ones and work from right to left.

- Add the ones.

- Add the tens.

- Add the hundreds, and so on.

▼ MATH TIP

To check an addition answer, switch the numbers and add again.

Example:

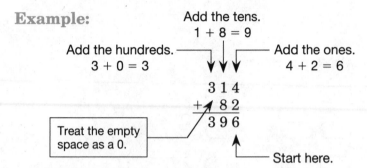

Add the tens.
1 + 8 = 9

Add the hundreds.
3 + 0 = 3

Add the ones.
4 + 2 = 6

```
 3 1 4
+  8 2
 3 9 6
```

Treat the empty space as a 0.

Start here.

Check:
```
    8 2
+ 3 1 4
  3 9 6 ✔
```

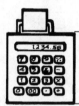

Calculator Solution of Example

Press Keys: (C) (3) (1) (4) (+) (8) (2) (=)

Answer: (3 9 6.)

▼ Practice

Add. Check each answer on scratch paper.

1.

12	50	$63	220	708	508
+ 6	+ 38	+ 25	+ 69	+ 291	+ 340

2.

$61	41	314	513	$3,036	6,102
24	33	203	242	801	2,321
+ 4	+ 24	+ 72	+ 133	+ 60	+ 562

3. What is the total weight of the three items shown at right?

3,423 lb.   1,015 lb.   350 lb.

Adding Numbers Written in a Row

To add numbers written in a row, write the numbers in a column and then add.

- Place the larger number on top.

- Line up the ones digits, tens digits, hundreds digits, and so on.

Example: Add 72 + 414   (row)

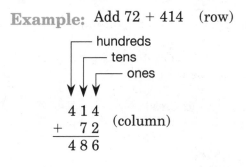

$$\begin{array}{r} 4\,1\,4 \\ +\quad 7\,2 \\ \hline 4\,8\,6 \end{array} \quad \text{(column)}$$

▼ **MATH TIP**

Line up the ones digits first. The other digits will line up automatically.

A. Your boss asks you to total the inventory items below. Add the number from each bin to find these totals.

	Inventoried Items	Bin A	Bin B	Bin C	Bin D	Total	
1.	pens	21	9	—	—	_____	pens
2.	rulers	9	—	30	—	_____	rulers
3.	erasers	20	—	48	111	_____	erasers
4.	ribbons (typewriter)	31	23	14	—	_____	ribbons
5.	pencils	10	12	22	34	_____	pencils
6.	envelopes	—	—	85	101	_____	envelopes
7.	paper (typewriter)	104	723	1,140	—	_____	paper
8.	folders	327	—	140	201	_____	folders

B. The four drivers that work at Short Distance Hauling keep track of their mileage. Add to find the total mileage of each driver during the four-day period shown.

Driver	Monday		Tuesday		Wednesday		Thursday	Total
1. W. Adams	203	+	215	+	100	+	80	_____
2. B. Carpenter	211	+	204	+	162	+	212	_____
3. C. Jansen	314	+	101	+	150	+	303	_____
4. D. Tracy	272	+	213	+	102	+	111	_____

Adding Dollars and Cents

Example 1: Add $5.17 and $2.42.

Line up the decimal points. From right to left, add the columns.

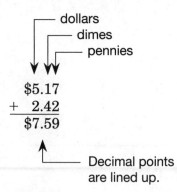

dollars

dimes

pennies

$5.17
+ 2.42
$7.59

Decimal points are lined up.

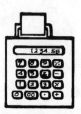

Calculator Solution of Example 1

Ⓒ ⑤ · ① ⑦ ⊕ ② · ④ ② ⊜

Answer: 7.59

Example 2: Add $2.27 and 71¢.

Step 1. Write 71¢ using a $.
71¢ = $0.71

Step 2. Add $2.27
+ 0.71
$2.98

Example 3: Add 53¢ and 42¢.
Write each sum in two ways.

As Cents	Using $
53¢	$0.53
+ 42¢	+ 0.42
95¢	$0.95

Add.

1.	$4.38	$2.37	$5.06
	+ 2.41	+ 0.51	3.41
			+ 0.32

2. $12.36 + $5.42 _____

3. $15.34 + $4.10 _____

4. $3.41 + $2.03 + $1.22 _____

5. $2.03 + $1.40 + $0.55 _____

6. $1.10 + $0.43 + $0.32 _____

7. $3.45 + 24¢ _____

8. 53¢ + 6¢ _____

9. $7.04 + 93¢ _____

Write each sum in two ways.

	As Cents	Using $
10. 85¢ + 14¢	_____	_____
11. 11¢ + 72¢	_____	_____
12. 63¢ + 34¢	_____	_____

Using the cents symbol, write the sum of each amount.
Then, write each sum using a dollar sign and decimal point.

13.

_85¢_ _____ _$0.85_ _____   _____ _____   _____ _____

14.

_____ _____   _____ _____   _____ _____

Using a dollar sign and decimal point, write each sum.

15.

_____   _____   _____

16.

_____   _____   _____

Choosing Information You Need

In real life, you often see lots of numbers and labels—sometimes many more than you care to!

What are labels? **Labels** are words (like pounds) and symbols (like $) that tell what numbers refer to.

- As your math skills increase, you'll learn to pick out just those numbers and labels you need in order to answer specific questions or perform specific tasks.

▼ Practice

Look at the sales ad at right, and choose an answer for each question below.

1. Which is the least expensive type of long-sleeve shirt?
   a) white
   b) western
   c) striped

2. Which is the most expensive type of short-sleeve shirt?
   a) plaid
   b) striped
   c) patterned

Problems 3–5 refer to the following additional information.

You decide to buy two short-sleeve striped shirts and one long-sleeve white shirt.

3. How many shirts do you plan to buy?
   a) 1
   b) 2
   c) 3

4. To determine how much you will spend, what amounts (necessary information) do you need to use?
   a) $12.90 and $13.29
   b) $10.20 and $13.29
   c) $10.20 and $12.90

5. What is the total cost of your purchase?
   a) $23.49
   b) $33.69
   c) $36.78

Carter's Annual Shirt Sale

Short-Sleeve Shirts

Plaid	Striped	Patterned
$11.75	$10.20	$12.49

Long-Sleeve Shirts

White	Western	Striped
$13.29	$16.70	$12.90

In problems 6–8, circle the answer choice for each A and B part. Then solve each problem.

6. Not counting tax, how much did Rhonda spend for lunch?

   A. What are you asked to find?
   a) the number of items bought
   b) amount spent for food items
   c) amount of Rhonda's bill

   B. What is the **necessary information?**
   a) $2.26, $0.60, and $0.23
   b) $2.00, $0.60, and $0.23
   c) $2.26, $2.00, and $0.60

Rhonda's Lunch Bill

Ham Sandwich	$2.26
Green Salad	2.00
Soft Drink	.60
Tax	.23
Total:	

7. At the Spring Sale, how much will Amy pay for a table and two matching chairs?

   A. What are you asked to find the cost of?
   a) one table and one chair
   b) one table and two chairs
   c) one table and three chairs

   B. What is the **necessary information?**
   a) $329 and $100
   b) $329 and $110
   c) $329 and $120

Armond Furniture SPRING SALE

Pecan Table	Oak Chair
$329	$110 each
Walnut Chair	Pecan Chair
$100 each	$120 each

8. Home sales in Oakdale for a six-month period are shown at right. How many homes were sold during the summer months?

   A. What is the **extra information?**
   a) 32, 46, and 51
   b) 46, 51, and 103
   c) 51, 46, and 124

   B. Which sum below gives the correct answer to question 8?

   a) 110   b) 103   c) 124
      124   110   110
   + 32   + 51   + 103

Month	Number Sold
June	103
July	110
August	124
January	32
February	46
March	51

Reading a Table

A table is a list of words and numbers written in labeled rows and columns.

- **Rows** are read from left to right.

- **Columns** are read from top to bottom.

Row: 15 29 25 →

Column: ↓ 35 17 43

Example: Look at the nutrition table below, and answer the questions.

Nutritional Values of Selected Meats
(Each value is for a six-ounce serving.)

Meat	Calories	Protein (g*)	Fat (g*)
Hamburger (lean)	370	47	19
Chicken (light)	280	54	6
Chicken (dark)	300	48	11
Ham (lean)	640	40	52
Lamb (lean)	480	43	32

*g = grams. A gram is a metric weight unit.
A raisin weighs about one gram.

---

1. How many grams of protein are contained in six ounces of lean ham?

   From left to right, scan the row labeled Ham (lean). Stop at the number that is also in the column labeled Protein.

   At the intersection of the Ham (lean) row and the Protein column is the number 40.

   Answer: 40 grams of protein

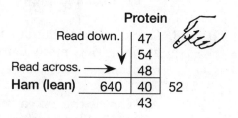

Protein
Read down. ↓ 47
54
Read across. → 48
Ham (lean)   640   40   52
43

2. Which of the listed meats is lowest in fat content?

   Scan down the column labeled Fat, and choose the smallest number: 6.

   Look left along the row containing the 6, and read that row's label.

   Answer: Chicken (light) has the lowest fat content: 6 grams per 6 ounces.

Read down. ↓ **Fat**
19
Chicken (light)   280   54   6
←   11
Look left   52
for label.   32

▼ Practice

Use the chart on page 40 to solve the problems below.

1. number of calories?

2. amount of protein?

3. amount of fat?

_____

_____

_____

According to the nutrition table, which six-ounce serving of meat has:

4. the largest number of calories?   _____

5. the smallest amount of protein?   _____

6. the largest amount of fat?   _____

Circle the correct answer.

7. Meat with a low fat content tends to have a high amount of _____.

    a) protein
    b) weight
    c) calories

8. Meat with a high calorie content tends to have a high amount of _____.

    a) protein
    b) fat
    c) weight

A large chicken salad contains 6 ounces of chicken light meat _and_ 6 ounces of chicken dark meat.

What is:

9. the total weight of the chicken?   _____

10. the total calorie content of the chicken?   _____

11. the total fat content of the chicken?   _____

Counting Calories

"This is the last straw!" exclaimed Sherry, tossing her swimsuit onto the bed. "Either this suit grows or I shrink!"

Right then and there, Sherry decided to go on a diet.

To prepare for her diet, Sherry read a book about food and calories. She learned that calories are a measure of food energy. And, she found out that eating unneeded calories makes you fat! Foods such as sweets have lots of calories but have very little food value. Foods such as green vegetables, though, are low in calories and are very good for you.

Sherry also discovered that lean meat and fish have as much food value as fatty meats but have far fewer calories.

Part of the information Sherry obtained is shown in the chart below.

Nutritional Information for Selected Fast Foods (Typical values are given.)			
Food Item	**Calories**	**Protein (g)**	**Fat (g)**
Hamburger	428	28	19
Cheeseburger	470	31	23
Fish Sandwich	344	33	10
Chicken Sandwich	378	32	12
French Fries (sm, lg)	170, 325	2, 4	7, 14
Soft Drink (sm, lg)	150, 300	0, 0	0, 0

▼ Practice

A. Answer these questions for Sherry.

> **The Combo**
>
> Cheeseburger
> Large Drink
> Large Fries

1. How many calories are contained in "The Combo" meal shown at right? _____

2. Which type of fast-food sandwich contains the least protein? _____ most fat? _____

3. List the four fast-food sandwiches by the number of calories each contains. List the sandwich with the least number first, and so on.

   1st _____ (least)
   2nd _____
   3rd _____
   4th _____ (most)

While shopping one Wednesday, Sherry ran into her friend Peggy. Peggy thought Sherry looked great and wanted to know the secret of her new diet.

"Cutting back on fast foods and watching my calories," said Sherry. "After shopping, I'll give you a copy of my typical daily meal plan."

"Thanks," said Peggy. "Maybe your good habits will rub off on me!"

Later, Sherry gave Peggy the meal plan shown at right.

B. Answer the following questions.

1. How many calories are contained in each of Sherry's typical meals?

Breakfast: _____

Lunch: _____

Dinner: _____

2. Of Sherry's three daily meals, which contains:

a) the most calories? _____

b) the least calories? _____

3. How many total calories are in Sherry's daily meal plan? _____

4. Using the numbers given in Sherry's daily meal plan, determine how many calories are in each of the following meals.

Food	Calories	Food	Calories
a) whole-grain cereal	_____	**b)** orange juice	_____
1 slice toast	_____	skim milk	_____
spinach	_____	cottage cheese	_____
baked potato	_____	broccoli	_____
coffee	_____	rice	_____
Total:	_____	**Total:**	_____

Typical Daily Meal Plan
Breakfast

Food	Calories
whole-grain cereal	115
orange juice	110
skim milk	100
1 slice toast, lightly buttered	100

Lunch

Food	Calories
cottage cheese	100
skim milk	100
broccoli	40
coffee	0

Dinner

Food	Calories
skim milk	100
chicken	300
baked potato	110
spinach	34
rice	103

Adding and Carrying

Adding larger numbers often involves **carrying**.

- To carry is to take a digit from the sum of one column and place it at the top of the column to the left.

> ▼ **MATH TIP**
>
> **Carrying** is also called **renaming** or **regrouping**.

Example: Add 57 and 26.

Step 1.

Add the ones: 7 + 6 = 13
(13 is 1 ten and 3 ones.)

┌ Carry 1 ten to top of tens column.

```
  1
  57
+ 26
  3
```

Step 2.

Add the tens: 1 + 5 + 2 = 8

┌ The carried 1 is added with the 5 and 2 in the tens column.

```
  1
  57
+ 26
  83
```

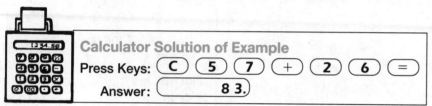

Calculator Solution of Example

Press Keys: (C) (5) (7) (+) (2) (6) (=)

Answer: (8 3.)

▼ Practice

Add. Complete each row of partially worked Skill Builders. Then solve the following problems.

Carrying to the Tens Column

Skill Builders				
1. 1 34 + 9 3	1 67¢ + 28¢ 5¢	1 53 + 47 0	1 42 36 + 8 6	2 $58 44 + 39 1

2.

```
  26        37¢        54        $79        65¢
+  9      + 19¢      + 48      + 27      + 28¢
```

3.

```
  34        27¢        52        46         86
   7        18¢        31        29         77
+  6      +  8¢      +  9      + 18      + 59
```

Carrying to the Hundreds Column

Skill Builders

Example

4.

	1		2	2
3 2 6	634	570	283	350
			172	286
+ 9 0	+ 85	+ 176	+ 64	+ 193
4 1 6	19	6	19	29

5.

$471	378	763	437	692
+ 84	+ 91	+ 170	+ 391	+ 285

6.

375	$482	253	$580	635
250	307	184	464	490
+ 43	+ 90	+ 71	+ 172	+ 293

Carrying to the Thousands Column

Skill Builders

Example

7.

	1		2	
6,3 6 2	5,825	7,900	5,725	8,850
			4,532	7,502
+ 8 3 5	+ 970	+ 1,376	+ 2,940	+ 5,644
7,1 9 7	795	76	197	96

8.

5,625	6,320	$3,890	8,732	7,500
+ 814	+ 940	+ 1,905	+ 4,850	+ 6,937

9.

2,750	3,935	5,244	6,815	$9,673
1,832	2,762	2,935	3,923	7,700
+ 412	+ 300	+ 1,410	+ 1,331	+ 5,925

Carrying to Two or More Columns

Sometimes you must carry to two or more columns.

Example: Add 486
              367
           +   95

Step 1.

```
   1
  4 8 6
  3 6 7
+   9 5
      8
```

Step 2.

```
  2 1
  4 8 6
  3 6 7
+   9 5
  9 4 8
```

Skill Builders

10.

```
 1 1              1            1 1            11            21
 172            468          2,947          374         2,685
+ 98          + 275          + 985          236         1,975
 ────          ─────          ─────          236        1,975
  70              3             32          + 159        +  850
                                             ─────        ─────
                                              69            10
```

11.

```
 546          $483          2,573          4,875          5,789
+ 84          + 278          + 984          + 1,766        + 2,643
```

12.

```
$356          285          1,475          4,496          5,784
 207          193            739          2,482          4,679
+ 93          + 108          + 568          + 1,757        + 2,875
```

---

13. You are a foreman on a construction site. Determine the total amount of rock that each employee of Emery Construction Company hauled in the loads reported below. All numbers are in pounds (lb.).

Emery Construction					
Load Number:	#1	#2	#3	#4	Total
Todd Burrell	1,538	979			_____
Joyce Dart	1,639	1,248	865		_____
Bill Jenkins	1,467	1,493	1,187		_____
Georgia Smith	1,566	1,378	1,078	948	_____
Luis Garcia	1,385	1,456	1,379	875	_____

Estimating Answers

Finding an exact answer takes time and effort! Luckily, many problems don't require an exact answer. A "close" answer or **estimate** will do fine.

Example: At a hardware sale, Alan bought the three items shown at right. How much did Alan pay in all? Choose answer a, b, or c.

a) $38.25 **b)** $43.75 **c)** $49.15

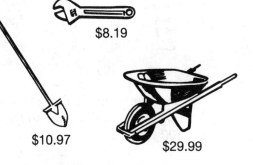

$8.19

$10.97

$29.99

Instead of finding an exact answer, estimate.

- To estimate, round each amount to the nearest dollar, and then add.

Exact	Estimate
$29.99	$30.00
10.97	11.00
+ 8.19	+ 8.00
	$49.00

▼ **MATH TIP**

Estimating is of great use
- anytime a close answer is all you need
- on math tests where answer choices are given

The $49.00 estimate tells you that choice *c* is correct. You do not need to find the exact answer.

Calculator Solution of Example
Estimation is also a good way to check a calculator answer.
An estimate tells if a calculator answer makes sense.

Press Keys: Ⓒ ② ⑨ ⊙ ⑨ ⑨ ⊕ ① ⓪ ⊙ ⑨ ⑦ ⊕ ⑧ ⊙ ① ⑨ ⊜

Answer: (49.15)

✔ Your estimate (49) is very close to the calculator answer.

▼ Practice

Estimate each sum below.

	Before adding, round to the	Estimate
1. 19¢ + 22¢ + 33¢	nearest dime	_____
2. 11 pens + 28 pens + 42 pens	nearest 10 pens	_____
3. $6.13 + $3.91 + $2.12	nearest dollar	_____
4. 289 miles + 193 miles + 414 miles	nearest 100 miles	_____
5. $4,950 + $3,175 + $1,910	nearest $1,000	_____

Using estimation, choose each correct answer.

6. How much for all three?
(Round each amount to the nearest dollar.)

   $27.79

$19.89 $9.85

a) $53.13
b) $57.53
c) $61.83
d) $64.23

7. How many miles did Sandi drive?
(Round each distance to the nearest
100 miles.)

a) 713
b) 833
c) 903
d) 1,003

Sandi's Mileage Record
Monday: 218 miles
Tuesday: 307 miles
Wednesday: 187 miles
Thursday: 291 miles

Compute both an estimate and an exact answer for
problems 8–10.

8. How many calories are in this meal? (Round each
amount to the nearest 100 calories.)

cheeseburger sandwich: 470 calories
one glass of whole milk: 206 calories
one piece of apple pie: 289 calories

_____   _____
   estimate   exact

9. What is the total attendance shown below? (Round each
amount to the nearest 1,000 people.)

Clinton High School
Weekend Baseball Games
Attendance Figures

Friday: 2,296
Saturday: 3,135
Sunday: 4,862

_____   _____
   estimate   exact

10. Brad bought a $489 desk, a $219 chair, and a $192
filing cabinet. How much did Brad spend in all?
(Round each amount to the nearest $100.)

_____   _____
   estimate   exact

Estimating and Shopping

Many people like to estimate while they shop. In this way, they have some idea of how much they are spending *before* they get to the cash register!

▼ Practice

Estimate the total spent in each shopping trip below. Round each amount to the nearest dollar before adding.

Grocery Costs

You Bought:	Actual Price	Estimate
1. milk	$1.93	_____
2. cereal	$3.38	_____
3. bread	$1.29	_____
4. jam	$3.08	_____
5. hamburger	$5.27	_____
6. flour	$3.80	_____
7. laundry soap	$6.99	_____
8. diapers	$11.89	_____
	Total:	_____

Clothing Costs

You Bought:	Actual Price	Estimate
1. shirt	$8.19	_____
2. socks	$3.88	_____
3. jeans	$15.49	_____
4. shorts	$11.75	_____
5. T-shirt	$7.77	_____
6. jacket	$39.88	_____
7. cap	$4.00	_____
8. shoes	$42.50	_____
	Total:	_____

Hardware Costs

You Bought:	Actual Price	Estimate
1. nails	$2.18	_____
2. hammer	$6.29	_____
3. wrench	$7.50	_____
4. shovel	$12.78	_____
5. rake	$10.35	_____
6. clamps	$4.80	_____
7. bolts	$2.75	_____
8. washers	$0.79	_____
	Total:	_____

Auto Parts Costs

You Bought:	Actual Price	Estimate
1. oil	$10.49	_____
2. wax	$3.99	_____
3. spark plugs	$7.06	_____
4. battery	$39.99	_____
5. brake fluid	$2.39	_____
6. ice scraper	$1.99	_____
7. tire	$69.50	_____
8. funnel	$3.49	_____
	Total:	_____

Carrying with Dollars and Cents

Carrying to the Dimes Column

Example 1: Add $6.23 and $2.49.

Line up the decimal points and add.

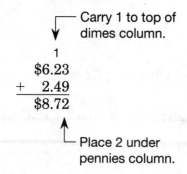

Carry 1 to top of dimes column.

```
   1
$6.23
+  2.49
$8.72
```

Place 2 under pennies column.

Carrying Across the Decimal Point

Example 2: Add $12.56 and $6.83.

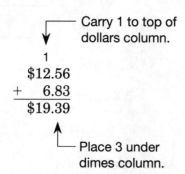

Carry 1 to top of dollars column.

```
    1
$12.56
+   6.83
$19.39
```

Place 3 under dimes column.

Example 3: Add $2.87 and 99¢.

Write 99¢ as $0.99 and add.

Carried 1s are placed at top of both dimes and dollars columns.

```
  1 1
$2.87
+  0.99
$3.86
```

Add.

1. $3.49 $5.38 $3.27
      + 1.37   + 0.98   1.19
                                  + 0.48

2. $7.28 + $3.19 _____

3. $4.34 + $0.38 _____

4. $2.29 + $1.49 + $0.99 _____

5. $5.53 $6.75 $3.58
      + 2.65   + 1.80   2.90
                                  + 1.81

6. $2.50 + $1.69 _____

7. $11.89 + $4.50 _____

8. $3.94 + $2.70 + $0.85 _____

9. $6.55 + $1.79 _____

10. $1.68 + 29¢ _____

11. $2.45 + 99¢ _____

12. $1.78 + 89¢ + 74¢ _____

Circle the best estimate, and then compute the actual price of each purchase below.

13. Customer buys:

$4.89   and $1.98

Best estimate: $6.00 or $7.00

Actual price: _____

16. Customer buys:

$1.39   and   49¢

Best estimate: $1.50 or $2.00

Actual price: _____

14. Customer buys:

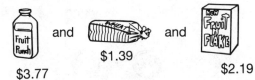

$3.77   and $1.39   and $2.19

Best estimate: $7.00 or $8.00

Actual price: _____

17. Customer buys:

$2.79   and $2.25   and $4.98

Best estimate: $9.00 or $10.00

Actual price: _____

15. Customer buys:

$317.49   and

$189.79

Best estimate: $400 or $500

Actual price: _____

18. Customer buys:

$6,243.99   and $2,045.25   and $985.50

Best estimate: $8,000 or $9,000

Actual price: _____

Adding Coins

Being able to add coins quickly is an important skill.

- Consumers use this skill to count change, to use a Laundromat, and to use a pay phone.

- Cashiers use this skill to count money received from customers and to give back change.

Adding Like Coins

- Count by 50s when you add 50¢ pieces:  +

| Count: | 50¢ | $1.00 | $1.50 | $2.00 |

- Count by 25s when you add quarters:

| Count: | 25¢ | 50¢ | 75¢ | $1.00 |

- Count by 10s when you add dimes:

| Count: | 10¢ | 20¢ | 30¢ | 40¢ | 50¢ |

- Count by 5s when you add nickels:

| Count: | 5¢ | 10¢ | 15¢ | 20¢ | 25¢ |

Example: Add the sum of money below.

Step 1. Choose a combination of coins that adds to $1.00.

Choose: 3 quarters + 2 dimes + 1 nickel
(Count: 25¢, 50¢, 75¢, 85¢, 95¢, $1.00)

Step 2. Add the remaining coins.

Add: 2 dimes + 1 nickel + 2 pennies
(Count: 10¢, 20¢, 25¢, 26¢, 27¢)

Answer: $1.27

▶ 52

▼ **MATH TIP**

To add a mixture of coins, group them into whole-dollar amounts whenever possible.

The circled coins total $1.00.
The other coins total 27¢.

▼ **Practice**

Find the sum of each group of coins.

1.  _____

2.  _____

3.  _____

4. _____

Find the sum of each group of coins. In each group, circle one
or two whole-dollar amounts.

5.  _____

7.  _____

6.  _____

8.  _____

9. What coins can you use to start a
washing machine that costs 90¢?

10. What coins can you use to place a $1.65
call in a pay phone?

Working with a Sales Bill

Marcy is a cashier at Jerry's Restaurant. Part of her job is to total each customer's bill and to take the customer's money. Most customers pay by cash, and Marcy has gotten pretty good with her money-counting skills.

Easy as her job sounds, Marcy tells her friends, "Working at Jerry's certainly isn't dull. You meet the real crazies!"

One Friday night, a young lady named Anna came to the register to pay her bill. Anna dumped the pile of money shown below on the counter and said, "This is all I have! It's either this or I guess I wash dishes!"

JERRY'S RESTAURANT				
Table No.	No. Persons	Bill No. 3792	Server No. 14	
1	hamburger		$1	69
1	large fries			79
1	medium soda			59
	Subtotal			
	Tax			15
	Total			

Anna's bill

▼ Practice

A. Help Marcy by answering these questions.

1. How much is Anna's bill? _____

2. How much money did Anna place on the counter? _____

3. Does Anna have enough money to pay her bill? _____

On one Saturday afternoon, Jason, a friend of Marcy's sister, walked up to the counter with a funny look in his eye.

Marcy couldn't believe what she saw. Somehow, Jason had spilled catsup all over his bill. "I was trying to do a trick," he said. "I slipped . . . sorry!"

Try as she could, Marcy was unable to read the dirtied bill. "Well, what did you have? I'll have to write another bill," Marcy said.

"A cheeseburger, a large 7-UP, a small fries, and a piece of cherry pie," replied Jason. "And, the pie was stale!"

Marcy took out a new bill and glanced at the menu.

Jerry's Restaurant			
Hamburger			$1.69
Cheeseburger			1.89
Chicken San.			2.19
Ham San.			2.09
		Small	Large
Fries		.59	.79
	Small	Medium	Large
Drinks	.44	.59	.74
Ice Cream		.69	.99
Pie			1.09

B. Do the following for Marcy.

1. Using the partial menu shown above, write Jason a new bill.

2. Write a tax of 22¢ on the bill.

3. Compute the total, and enter this amount on the bill.

JERRY'S RESTAURANT				
Table No.	No. Persons	Bill No.	Server No.	
	Subtotal			
	Tax			
	Total			

Jason's new bill

Putting It All Together

Completing a Catalog Order Form

Look at this sample catalog page.

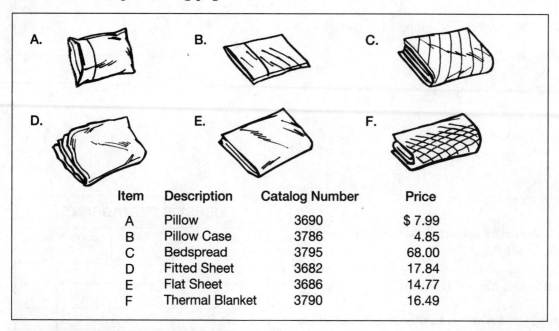

Item	Description	Catalog Number	Price
A	Pillow	3690	$ 7.99
B	Pillow Case	3786	4.85
C	Bedspread	3795	68.00
D	Fitted Sheet	3682	17.84
E	Flat Sheet	3686	14.77
F	Thermal Blanket	3790	16.49

▼ Practice

In this exercise, you will review what you have learned about adding whole numbers and money amounts.

1. You want to order one of each catalog item. List these six items on the order form *in the order of catalog number*. (List the item with lowest catalog number first, and so on.)

Catalog Order Form

	Catalog Number	Description	Price
1.	3682	Fitted Sheet	$17.84
2.			
3.			
4.			
5.			
6.			
		Subtotal:	
		Amount of Tax:	
		Total Cost:	

2. Compute the total cost of the six items before tax. Write this total in the space labeled Subtotal.

3. Use the partial tax table below, and determine the amount of tax on your purchase. Write this amount in the space labeled Amount of Tax.

Amount of Sale	Tax	Amount of Sale	Tax
$28.70 to $28.89	$1.44	$129.30 to $129.49	$6.47
28.90 to 29.09	1.45	129.50 to 129.69	6.48
29.10 to 29.29	1.46	129.70 to 129.89	6.49
29.30 to 29.49	1.47	129.90 to 130.09	6.50
29.50 to 29.69	1.48	130.10 to 130.29	6.51
29.70 to 29.89	1.49	130.30 to 130.49	6.52

4. Add the Subtotal and the Amount of Tax to determine your total cost. Write this amount in the space labeled Total Cost.

5. Imagine that your neighbor wants to order a pillow, a pillow case, and a thermal blanket from the same catalog.

a) Fill out the order form below for your neighbor. List the purchased items in order of catalog number—as you did on page 56.

b) Fill in the three amounts indicated: Subtotal, Amount of Tax, and Total Cost. Use the partial tax table in problem 3 above.

Catalog Order Form

	Catalog Number	Description	Price
1.			
2.			
3.			
4.			
5.			
6.			
		Subtotal:	
		Amount of Tax:	
		Total Cost:	

Subtraction

Some expenses occur when you least expect them.

Late Saturday night, Justine finally finished paying her bills and balancing her checkbook. Wearily she thought to herself, "No matter how much money I bring home, it always seems as if I owe more than I make. When it comes to money, I use a lot more minus signs than plus signs!"

Think About It

• Do you feel the way Justine does? Take a few moments to imagine all the times Justine subtracts money in her life. Jot down as many of these situations as you can.

• Do you think it's true that people subtract money more often than they add it?

How Does Subtraction Play a Part in *Your* Life?

Describe two times in the past month when you subtracted one number from another.

1) _____

2) _____

If subtracting numbers is a part of your job, tell how.

_____

_____

Have you ever used a calculator for subtracting? Describe the situation.

_____

_____

Have you ever estimated when faced with a subtraction problem? What did you do?

_____

_____

Can you think of a time when subtraction was particularly difficult? Why was it hard?

_____

_____

Skills You Will Learn

Number Skills
- simple subtracting
- subtracting by borrowing
- subtracting dollars and cents

Life and Workplace Skills
- understanding a paycheck stub
- interpreting a charge-card statement
- keeping track of charge-card spending
- counting correct change
- balancing a checkbook
- recording transactions in a savings account

Thinking Skills
- subtracting and estimating
- figuring change by "counting up"

Calculator Skills
- subtracting whole numbers
- subtracting dollars and cents
- avoiding keying errors

Subtracting Small Numbers

To **subtract** is to take away. Another word for subtract is
minus. As shown in the example, the **subtract** (or **minus**)
sign (−) indicates subtraction.

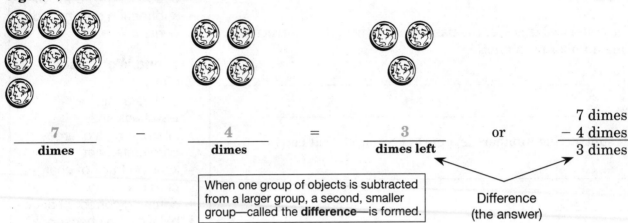

7	−	4	=	3	or	7 dimes
dimes		**dimes**		**dimes left**		− 4 dimes
						3 dimes

> When one group of objects is subtracted
> from a larger group, a second, smaller
> group—called the **difference**—is formed.

Difference
(the answer)

▼ Practice

Write numbers for the following subtractions.

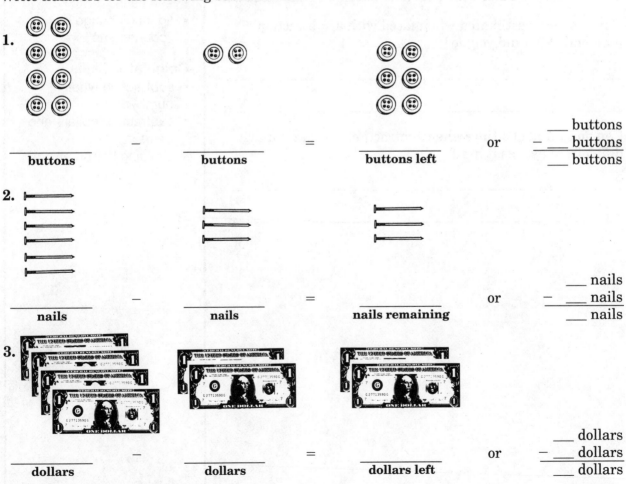

1.

	−		=		or	___ buttons
buttons		**buttons**		**buttons left**		− ___ buttons
						___ buttons

2.

	−		=		or	___ nails
nails		**nails**		**nails remaining**		− ___ nails
						___ nails

3.

	−		=		or	___ dollars
dollars		**dollars**		**dollars left**		− ___ dollars
						___ dollars

Addition and subtraction are closely related. The examples below show how to think of subtraction in terms of addition.

▼ **MATH TIP**

To simplify subtraction, think of subtracting as "undoing" addition.

Examples:

To Solve:	You Think:	In Words:	Answer:
$9 - 6$	$6 +$ _____ $= 9$	6 plus *what number* equals 9?	3
$\$18 - \$9$	$\$9 +$ _____ $= \$18$	$9 plus *how many dollars* equals $18?	$9

Write each answer on the line provided.

	To Solve:	You Think:	To Solve:	You Think:
4.	$8 - 3$	$3 + \underline{\ 5\ } = 8$	$9¢ - 5¢$	$5¢ +$ _____ $= 9¢$
5.	$7 - 2$	$2 +$ _____ $= 7$	$5 - 2$	$2 +$ _____ $= 5$
6.	$\$6 - \$4$	$\$4 +$ _____ $= \$6$	$9 - 7$	$7 +$ _____ $= 9$
7.	$17 - 8$	$8 +$ _____ $= 17$	$15¢ - 7¢$	$7¢ +$ _____ $= 15¢$
8.	$16¢ - 9¢$	$9¢ +$ _____ $= 16¢$	$12 - 8$	$8 +$ _____ $= 12$
9.	$15 - 9$	$9 +$ _____ $= 15$	$\$14 - \$7$	$\$7 +$ _____ $= \$14$

▼ Practice

Subtract. The top numbers are smaller than 10.

10.	$\begin{array}{r} 7 \\ -\ 5 \\ \hline 2 \end{array}$	$\begin{array}{r} 8 \\ -\ 3 \\ \hline \end{array}$	$\begin{array}{r} 9 \\ -\ 3 \\ \hline \end{array}$	$\begin{array}{r} 4 \\ -\ 0 \\ \hline \end{array}$	$\begin{array}{r} \$9 \\ -\ 7 \\ \hline \end{array}$	$\begin{array}{r} 7 \\ -\ 3 \\ \hline \end{array}$
11.	$\begin{array}{r} 8 \\ -\ 4 \\ \hline \end{array}$	$\begin{array}{r} 9¢ \\ -\ 5¢ \\ \hline \end{array}$	$\begin{array}{r} 7 \\ -\ 2 \\ \hline \end{array}$	$\begin{array}{r} 8 \\ -\ 6 \\ \hline \end{array}$	$\begin{array}{r} 6 \\ -\ 2 \\ \hline \end{array}$	$\begin{array}{r} \$5 \\ -\ 4 \\ \hline \end{array}$
12.	$\begin{array}{r} 5 \\ -\ 5 \\ \hline \end{array}$	$\begin{array}{r} 9 \\ -\ 6 \\ \hline \end{array}$	$\begin{array}{r} \$5 \\ -\ 2 \\ \hline \end{array}$	$\begin{array}{r} 7 \\ -\ 4 \\ \hline \end{array}$	$\begin{array}{r} 8 \\ -\ 5 \\ \hline \end{array}$	$\begin{array}{r} 7 \\ -\ 2 \\ \hline \end{array}$

Subtract. The top numbers are 10 or larger.

13.

10	12¢	14	17	11	13
− 3	− 9¢	− 6	− 8	− 4	− 9

14.

$11	14	15	16¢	14	15
− 8	− 9	− 6	− 7¢	− 5	− 9

15.

13	$14	18	15	17	14¢
− 4	− 7	− 9	− 7	− 9	− 8¢

16. In A and B, match a difference in the second column with an equal difference in the first column.

A.	
__h__ **1.** 9 − 7	**a)** 8 − 1
_____ **2.** 7 − 3	**b)** 9 − 3
_____ **3.** 4 − 4	**c)** 4 − 1
_____ **4.** 8 − 5	**d)** 9 − 4
_____ **5.** 6 − 1	**e)** 8 − 4
_____ **6.** 7 − 6	**f)** 8 − 8
_____ **7.** 9 − 2	**g)** 6 − 5
_____ **8.** 8 − 2	**h)** 7 − 5

B.	
__f__ **1.** 18 − 9	**a)** 12 − 9
_____ **2.** 13 − 9	**b)** 15 − 8
_____ **3.** 10 − 8	**c)** 14 − 9
_____ **4.** 11 − 8	**d)** 12 − 8
_____ **5.** 14 − 8	**e)** 11 − 9
_____ **6.** 14 − 7	**f)** 17 − 8
_____ **7.** 10 − 2	**g)** 12 − 6
_____ **8.** 12 − 7	**h)** 13 − 5

Subtracting Two or More Numbers

To subtract two or more numbers:

- First, subtract the second number from the first number.

- Then, subtract the next number from the answer, and so on.

Example: $17 − 8 − 5 = 4$

$$17 - 8 - 5 = 4$$

17. $19 − 7 − 6 =$ $14 − $3 − $9 =$ $17 − 9 − 5 =$

18. $16 − 8 − 5 =$ $12 − 7 − 5 =$ $18¢ − 7¢ − 8¢ =$

Calculator Subtraction

Subtracting One Number from Another

* The **subtract key** $\ominus$ is used to subtract one number from another.

Example 1: To subtract 68 from 117 on your calculator, press keys as shown at right.

Answer: 49

Press Keys	Display Reads
C	0.
1 1 7	1 1 7.
−	1 1 7.
6 8	6 8.
=	4 9.

Subtracting Two or More Numbers

To subtract two or more numbers:

* Enter each number and then press $\ominus$.
* Press $\equiv$ only after entering the final number.

▼ **MATH TIP**

Remember that the number being subtracted must come *after* the minus sign.
117 − 68 is *not* the same as 68 − 117.

Example 2: You paid for the following items with a $10 bill. How much change should you receive?

$3.79   and $2.49

To solve, subtract the first amount from $10.00 and the second amount from the remaining amount.
   $10.00 − $3.79 − $2.49

Answer: $3.72

Press Keys	Display Reads
C	0.
1 0 · 0 0	1 0 . 0 0
−	1 0 . 0 0
3 · 7 9	3 . 7 9
−	6 . 2 1
2 · 4 9	2 . 4 9
=	3 . 7 2

▼ **MATH TIP**

$10 can be entered as 10 or as 10.00. Many people prefer to enter the extra 0s as a reminder that they are working with dollars and cents.

Calculator Discovery

Try the following problem on your calculator:

	You Subtract	**The Display Reads**
	$0.56 - $0.26	0.3

You don't need to enter the initial zero before the decimal.

The answer is $0.30, but the display reads 0.3.

• A calculator does not display a 0 that is at the right-hand end of the decimal part of an answer.

Write your answer as $0.30, not $0.3.

▼ Practice

A. Fill in the key symbols to show how to calculate each answer.

Example: 97 − 49   (C)(9)(7)(−)(4)(9)(=)

1. 174 − 89   ( )( )( )( )( )( )( )

2. $25.00 − $19.78   ( )( )( )( )( )( )( )( )( )( )( )( )

3. $1.87 − $0.97   ( )( )( )( )( )( )( )( )( )( )

4. 2,386 − 1,579   ( )( )( )( )( )( )( )( )( )( )

B. Solve these problems on your calculator.

1.
32	56	$3.00	$5.78	3,423
− 9	− 38	− 1.73	− 2.88	− 1,970

2. 84 − 39 − 8   247 − 179 − 37   837 − 384 − 219

3. $10.00 − $4.89 − $3.01 $20.00 − $8.89 − $4.51

4. Use your calculator to subtract Phil's expenses from the amount he received for a carpeting job. (Amount received − expenses = profit)

Expense Sheet		
Amount Received:	$ 650.00	
	− 390.74	← materials
	− 45.91	← new tools
	− 75.00	← assistant
	− 4.50	← gas
Profit:	$	

Keying Errors

Called "keying errors," calculator errors are very common. In fact, keying errors are so common that we want to take this page to alert you to them.

Below are three types of keying errors:

- pressing the wrong key

  Example: Pressing (5)(1) instead of (4)(1).

- double keying—accidentally pressing the same key twice

  Example: Pressing (3)(3)(5) instead of (3)(5).

- transposing digits—pressing keys in the wrong order

  Example: Pressing (8)(2) instead of (2)(8).

As you use your calculator in this book, be careful to avoid each type of keying error.

C. For each problem below, indicate by a check (✓) which type of error was made. Then, fill in the blank keys to show the correct way to key each problem.

Problem To Solve	Keys Pressed	Wrong Key	Double Keying	Transposed Digits
1. 38 + 19	(C)(3)(8)(8)(+)(1)(9)(=)	___	___	___
Correct:	( )( )( )( )( )( )			
2. 62 − 43	(C)(6)(2)(−)(3)(4)(=)	___	___	___
Correct:	( )( )( )( )( )( )			
3. 94 + 58	(C)(9)(4)(+)(4)(8)(=)	___	___	___
Correct:	( )( )( )( )( )( )			
4. $.87 + $.29	(C)(·)(7)(8)(+)(·)(2)(9)(=)	___	___	___
Correct:	( )( )( )( )( )( )( )			
5. 75 + 46	(C)(7)(5)(−)(4)(6)(=)	___	___	___
Correct:	( )( )( )( )( )( )			

Subtracting Larger Numbers

When subtracting larger numbers, start with the ones and work from right to left:

- Subtract the ones.

- Subtract the tens.

- Subtract the hundreds, and so on.

MATH TIP

Check a subtraction problem by adding the answer to the bottom number. The sum should equal the top number.

Example:

Subtract the tens.
$9 - 4 = 5$

Subtract the hundreds.
$8 - 5 = 3$

Subtract the ones.
$3 - 1 = 2$

$$
\begin{array}{r}
8\,9\,3 \\
-\ 5\,4\,1 \\
\hline
3\,5\,2
\end{array}
$$

Start here.

Check by Adding:

$$
\begin{array}{r}
541 \quad \text{(bottom number)} \\
+\ 352 \quad \text{(answer)} \\
\hline
893 \quad \text{(top number)}
\end{array}
$$

Calculator Solution of Example

Press Keys: (C) (8) (9) (3) (−) (5) (4) (1) (=)

Answer: (3 5 2.)

▼ Practice

Subtract. Check each answer on scratch paper.

1.

35¢	44	58	62¢	29	73
− 24¢	− 20	− 45	− 11¢	− 13	− 50

2.

187	168	$195	157	280	354
− 64	− 50	− 75	− 106	− 150	− 123

3.

$675	840	1,875	2,966	$3,489	5,760
− 342	− 430	− 650	− 2,425	− 1,357	− 2,430

4. How much heavier is the pickup than the sports car pictured at right?

_____

3,694 lb.   2,593 lb.

Subtracting Numbers Written in a Row

To subtract numbers written in a row, write the numbers in a column and then subtract.

- Place the larger number on top.

- Line up the ones digits, tens digits, hundreds digits, and so on.

Example: Subtract: 1,768 − 530 (row)

```
           ones
           ↓
   1,7 6 8   (column)
 −   5 3 0
   1,2 3 8
```

5. **A.** Imagine that you are a record keeper for a trucking company. As each loaded truck leaves the company yard, you record its weight. As shown below, by subtracting column b from column a, you can compute the weight of gravel in each truck. Complete the "Gravel Weight" column below.

▼ **REMINDER**

Line up the ones digits first. Then the other digits will line up automatically.

	Truck	Loaded Weight (a)*	Empty Weight (b)*	Gravel Weight (a − b)*
1.	M194	7,987	4,980	_3,007_
2.	M207	8,865	5,025	_____
3.	M451	6,787	4,335	_____
4.	M560	7,759	4,500	_____
5.	M800	7,986	4,720	_____

*All weights are given in pounds.

B. As a manager at Super Foods Warehouse, one of your responsibilities is to order more products when necessary. By subtracting column b from column a on an inventory form, you can determine how much of each listed item to order. Complete the "To Order" column below.

Inventory Form			
Food Item	Full-Shelf Amount (a)	Presently on Hand (b)	To Order (a − b)
1. Peas	3,980 cans	830 cans	_3,150_ cans
2. Corn	2,929 cans	435 cans	_____ cans
3. Pickles	1,867 gal.	54 gal.	_____ gal.
4. Mayonnaise	4,748 jars	627 jars	_____ jars
5. Soap	976 boxes	43 boxes	_____ boxes

Subtracting Dollars and Cents

Example 1: Subtract: $8.69 − $2.32

Line up the decimal points. From right to left, subtract the columns.

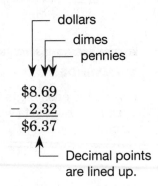

dollars
dimes
pennies

$8.69
− 2.32
$6.37

↑ Decimal points are lined up.

Answer: $6.37

Example 2: Subtract 54¢ from $3.89.

Step 1. Write 54¢ as a decimal.
54¢ = $0.54

Step 2. Subtract: $3.89
− .54
$3.35

Answer: $3.35

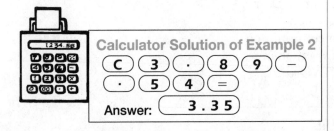

Calculator Solution of Example 2

C 3 . 8 9 −
. 5 4 =

Answer: 3 . 3 5

Example 3: Subtract 27¢ from 79¢.
Write your answer in two ways.

As Cents	Using $
79¢	$0.79
− 27¢	− 0.27
52¢	$0.52

Answer: 52¢ or $0.52

▼ Practice

Subtract.

1. $5.74 $8.62 $9.99
   − 3.12   − 2.00   − 5.79

2. $16.75 − $5.00 _____

3. $27.85 − $12.35 _____

4. $8.79 − $3.25 − $2.10 _____

5. $1.97 − 45¢ _____

6. $2.99 − 89¢ _____

7. $4.75 − 50¢ _____

8. $5.95 − $2.25 − 50¢ _____

9. $1.88 − 64¢ − 13¢ _____

Write each answer in two ways.

	As Cents	Using $
10. 82¢ − 60¢	22¢	$0.22
11. 78¢ − 45¢	_____	_____
12. 98¢ − 57¢	_____	_____

Subtracting Coins

To subtract coins, take away the coins you're subtracting.
Then, count the remaining coins.

Example: How much is left if you spend 61¢?

Step 1.

Take Away

Step 2.

Count

61¢ is
crossed out.

32¢ is left.

▼ Practice

How much is left if you:

1. spend 50¢? _____

3. take away 85¢? _____

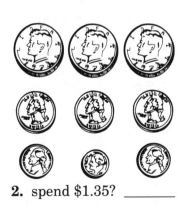

2. spend $1.35? _____

4. give away $1.60? _____

Understanding a Paycheck Stub

When an employer pays you, you are given both a paycheck and a paycheck stub. The stub tells your:

- **gross pay**—the amount you actually earned

- **net pay**—the amount of your paycheck (take-home pay)

- **deductions**—amounts withheld from your paycheck by your employer

> Net Pay = Gross Pay − Total Deductions

Look at the example paycheck stub below, and answer the questions on the next page.

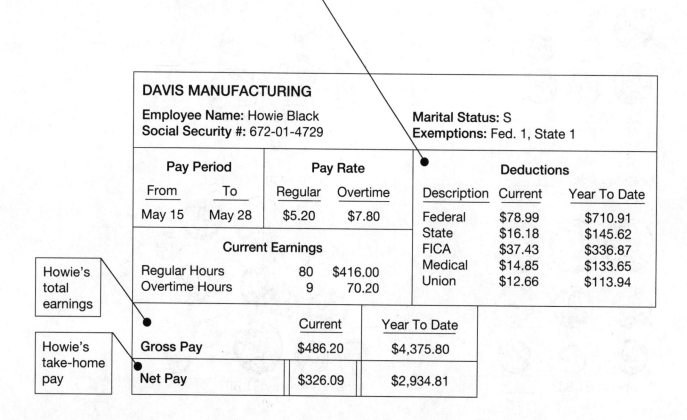

Types of Deductions

- Federal: an amount withheld for federal (U.S. government) taxes

- State: an amount withheld for state taxes

- FICA (**F**ederal **I**nsurance **C**ontributions **A**ct): an amount withheld for social security

- Medical: employee's share of medical insurance

- Union: employee's contributions to a union (only for employees belonging to a union)

DAVIS MANUFACTURING

Employee Name: Howie Black
Social Security #: 672-01-4729

Marital Status: S
Exemptions: Fed. 1, State 1

Pay Period		Pay Rate		Deductions		
From	To	Regular	Overtime	Description	Current	Year To Date
May 15	May 28	$5.20	$7.80	Federal	$78.99	$710.91
				State	$16.18	$145.62
Current Earnings				FICA	$37.43	$336.87
Regular Hours		80	$416.00	Medical	$14.85	$133.65
Overtime Hours		9	70.20	Union	$12.66	$113.94

Howie's total earnings

Howie's take-home pay

	Current	Year To Date
Gross Pay	$486.20	$4,375.80
Net Pay	$326.09	$2,934.81

A. Fill in each blank with a number taken from Howie's paycheck stub.

    1. For each "regular hour" of work, Howie earns _____.
       (regular pay rate)

    2. For each hour of overtime, Howie earns _____.
       (overtime pay rate)

    3. During this pay period, Howie earned _____.
       (gross pay)

    4. For this pay period, Howie takes home _____.
       (net pay)

    5. Howie's largest current deduction is _____.

    6. What two ways can Howie use to compute his total deductions for this pay period?

       a) add: _____ + _____ + _____ + _____ + _____

       b) subtract: _____ − _____
         (gross pay − net pay)

B. Compute an answer to each problem below.

    1. For each hour of work, how much more does Howie earn
       during overtime than during regular time?
       (overtime rate − regular rate)

    2. How many total hours did Howie work this pay period?
       (regular hours plus overtime hours)

    3. During this pay period, how much more did Howie pay
       in federal taxes than in state taxes?
       (federal taxes − state taxes)

    4. Add to determine the total amount of Howie's
       deductions for this pay period.
       (add the five listed deductions)

    5. Compute Howie's total deductions by subtracting net
       pay from gross pay. Is your answer the same as the
       answer you computed in problem 4?

Interpreting a Charge-Card Statement

You have probably heard the expression, "Pay with plastic!" To "pay with plastic" means to charge a purchase on a **charge card**.

At the end of the month, the charge-card company sends the card holder a **statement**. This statement lists new purchases and has a summary of the amount the card holder owes. A sample charge-card statement is shown below.

the amount owed when the previous statement was issued

purchases and cash withdrawals made since the last statement

money paid since the last statement

the value of returned merchandise

a monthly charge based on the amount owed the card company

the amount now owed

	Previous Balances	New Purchases and Advances	Payments	Credits	FINANCE CHARGES	New Balances
Purchases	175.25	96.84	100.00	32.12	1.13	141.10
Cash Advances	.00	20.00	.00	.00	.00	20.00
Total	175.25	116.84	100.00	32.12	1.13	161.10

Statement Date	# of Days in Statement Period	Date Payment Due	To avoid additional FINANCE CHARGES on the New Balance of Purchases, pay the full amount by the Date Payment Due. If the full amount is not paid, FINANCE CHARGES will be incurred.
6/1	31	6/14	

Account Number	Credit Limit		FINANCE CHARGES are incurred on the Average Daily Principal Balance of cash advances from date posted to your account until payment in full is entered to your account.
	Total	Unused	NOTICE: See Reverse Side for important information.
287-600-12	2,000	1,839	

▼ Practice

Check the amounts on the charge-card statement. Take all numbers from the row labeled "Total," and do the following.

1. Compute the sum: Previous Balances + New Purchases and Advances + Finance Charges _____

2. Compute the sum: Payments + Credits   _____

3. Subtract answer 2 from answer 1.   _____

4. Does answer 3 equal the amount listed as
   the Total New Balances on the statement?   _____

Keeping Track of Charge-Card Spending

Jan Brooks used to have a spending problem. Like many people, Jan
uses a charge card. And, like many people, Jan is always surprised at
the amount of her bill at the end of each month!

To help control her spending, Jan now keeps a record of her charges.
She keeps a record in a notebook at home. By keeping track of
expenses in this way, Jan has managed to budget her monthly income
much better.

A page from her notebook is shown below.

Date	Description	Charges	Payments and Credits	Balance Owed
4/1	Beginning Balance			$376.81
4/3	New Hat (Hat Shoppe)	$12.99		
4/6	Gasoline (Towne Gas)	$11.75		
4/9	Payment		$100.00	
4/11	Groceries (Best Food Store)	$44.85		
4/13	Return of Blouse (Credit)		$23.20	
4/24	Gasoline (Robert's)	$13.00		
4/25	Payment		$120.00	
4/27	Medical Supplies	$27.50		

▼ Practice

1. Fill in the **balance owed** after each entry recorded in
   Jan's book.

2. What total amount did Jan charge during April?

3. How much in total payments did Jan make during April?

4. Not counting finance charges, how much was Jan able to
   decrease her **balance owed** during April? (Hint: Subtract
   the 4/27 balance from the 4/1 balance.)

Subtracting by Borrowing

When a digit in the bottom number is larger than the digit above it, you must **borrow** in order to subtract.

The example below shows how to borrow from the tens in order to subtract the ones.

▼ MATH TIP

Borrowing is also called **renaming** or **regrouping**.

Example: Subtract

$$\begin{array}{r} 8\,2 \\ -\ 3\,7 \end{array}$$ ← 2 is smaller than 7, so you must borrow in order to subtract.

Step 1.
$$\begin{array}{r} 7 \\ \not8\,2 \\ -\ 3\,7 \end{array}$$
— 8 is replaced by 7. (1 ten is borrowed.)

Step 2.
$$\begin{array}{r} 7\,12 \\ \not8\,\not2 \\ -\ 3\,7 \end{array}$$
— The borrowed 10 is added to the 2 to give 12 ones.

Step 3.
$$\begin{array}{r} 7\,12 \\ \not8\,\not2 \\ -\ 3\,7 \\ \hline 4\,5 \end{array}$$
Subtract each column:
- ones: $12 - 7 = 5$
- tens: $7 - 3 = 4$

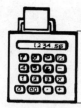

Calculator Solution of Example

Press Keys: (C) (8) (2) (−) (3) (7) (=)

Answer: (45.)

▼ Practice

Subtract. Complete each row of partially worked Skill Builders. Then solve the following problems.

Borrowing from the Tens Column

Skill Builders				
1. $\begin{array}{r} {}^{2\,15} \\ \not3\not5 \\ -\ 7 \\ \hline 8 \end{array}$	$\begin{array}{r} {}^{1\,14} \\ \not2\not4 \\ -\ 9 \\ \hline \end{array}$	$\begin{array}{r} {}^{3\,16} \\ \not4\not6 \\ -\ 2\,7 \\ \hline 9 \end{array}$	$\begin{array}{r} {}^{6\,13} \\ \not7\not3 \\ -\ 3\,8 \\ \hline \end{array}$	$\begin{array}{r} {}^{4\,15} \\ 2\not5\not5 \\ -\ 3\,9 \\ \hline 6 \end{array}$
2. $\begin{array}{r} 34¢ \\ -\ 6¢ \\ \hline \end{array}$	$\begin{array}{r} 42 \\ -\ 8 \\ \hline \end{array}$	$\begin{array}{r} 57 \\ -\ 29 \\ \hline \end{array}$	$\begin{array}{r} 72¢ \\ -\ 37¢ \\ \hline \end{array}$	$\begin{array}{r} 84 \\ -\ 56 \\ \hline \end{array}$
3. $\begin{array}{r} 50 \\ -\ 32 \\ \hline \end{array}$	$\begin{array}{r} \$37 \\ -\ 19 \\ \hline \end{array}$	$\begin{array}{r} 287 \\ -\ 69 \\ \hline \end{array}$	$\begin{array}{r} 351 \\ -\ 48 \\ \hline \end{array}$	$\begin{array}{r} 413 \\ -\ 208 \\ \hline \end{array}$

Borrowing from the Hundreds Column

Skill Builders

Example

4.

$$\begin{array}{r}\overset{3\;11}{4\,\cancel{1}\,3} \\ -7\,2 \\ \hline 3\,4\,1\end{array}\qquad\begin{array}{r}\overset{6\;15}{7\,\cancel{5}\,4} \\ -9\,0 \\ \hline 4\end{array}\qquad\begin{array}{r}\overset{2\;12}{3\,\cancel{2}\,9} \\ -8\,7 \\ \hline 2\end{array}\qquad\begin{array}{r}\overset{7\;12}{8\,\cancel{2}\,6} \\ -2\,7\,4 \\ \hline 5\,2\end{array}\qquad\begin{array}{r}\overset{4\;16}{5\,\cancel{6}\,8} \\ -3\,9\,5 \\ \hline 3\end{array}$$

5.

$$\begin{array}{r}\$638 \\ -85 \\ \hline\end{array}\qquad\begin{array}{r}273 \\ -91 \\ \hline\end{array}\qquad\begin{array}{r}427 \\ -60 \\ \hline\end{array}\qquad\begin{array}{r}\$739 \\ -77 \\ \hline\end{array}\qquad\begin{array}{r}365 \\ -83 \\ \hline\end{array}$$

6.

$$\begin{array}{r}284 \\ -193 \\ \hline\end{array}\qquad\begin{array}{r}341 \\ -150 \\ \hline\end{array}\qquad\begin{array}{r}709 \\ -173 \\ \hline\end{array}\qquad\begin{array}{r}442 \\ -261 \\ \hline\end{array}\qquad\begin{array}{r}\$538 \\ -285 \\ \hline\end{array}$$

Borrowing from the Thousands Column

Skill Builders

Example

7.

$$\begin{array}{r}\overset{1\;15}{2,\cancel{5}\,4\,7} \\ -9\,3\,2 \\ \hline 1,6\,1\,5\end{array}\qquad\begin{array}{r}\overset{0\;15}{1,\cancel{5}\,7\,5} \\ -8\,5\,4 \\ \hline 2\,1\end{array}\qquad\begin{array}{r}\overset{3\;14}{4,\cancel{4}\,2\,5} \\ -9\,1\,5 \\ \hline 1\,0\end{array}\qquad\begin{array}{r}\overset{4\;12}{5,\cancel{2}\,8\,0} \\ -1,7\,5\,0 \\ \hline 3\,0\end{array}\qquad\begin{array}{r}\overset{6\;16}{7,\cancel{6}\,2\,5} \\ -2,8\,1\,4 \\ \hline 1\,1\end{array}$$

8.

$$\begin{array}{r}5,397 \\ -750 \\ \hline\end{array}\qquad\begin{array}{r}2,384 \\ -954 \\ \hline\end{array}\qquad\begin{array}{r}\$7,291 \\ -340 \\ \hline\end{array}\qquad\begin{array}{r}5,021 \\ -900 \\ \hline\end{array}\qquad\begin{array}{r}2,592 \\ -781 \\ \hline\end{array}$$

9.

$$\begin{array}{r}\$5,284 \\ -1,940 \\ \hline\end{array}\qquad\begin{array}{r}3,194 \\ -2,752 \\ \hline\end{array}\qquad\begin{array}{r}7,298 \\ -2,355 \\ \hline\end{array}\qquad\begin{array}{r}\$6,842 \\ -2,920 \\ \hline\end{array}\qquad\begin{array}{r}\$7,500 \\ -2,700 \\ \hline\end{array}$$

Borrowing from Two or More Columns

Sometimes you must borrow from two or more columns.

Example: Subtract

$$\begin{array}{r} 526 \\ -\ 139 \end{array}$$

Step 1.

$$\begin{array}{r} 5\ \overset{1\ 16}{2\ 6} \\ -\ 1\ 3\ 9 \\ \hline 7 \end{array}$$

Step 2.

$$\begin{array}{r} \overset{4\ 11\ 16}{5\ 2\ 6} \\ -\ 1\ 3\ 9 \\ \hline 3\ 8\ 7 \end{array}$$

Skill Builders

10.

$$\begin{array}{r} \overset{5\ 12\ 14}{6\ 3\ 4} \\ -\ \ \ 7\ 5 \\ \hline 5\ 9 \end{array}$$

$$\begin{array}{r} \overset{2\ 16\ 11}{3\ 7\ 1} \\ -\ \ \ 9\ 3 \\ \hline 8 \end{array}$$

$$\begin{array}{r} \overset{7\ 12}{4\ 8\ 2} \\ -\ 1\ 9\ 5 \\ \hline 7 \end{array}$$

$$\begin{array}{r} \overset{12\ 13\ 17}{1,3\ 4\ 7} \\ -\ \ \ 9\ 6\ 8 \\ \hline 9 \end{array}$$

$$\begin{array}{r} \overset{5\ 11\ 12}{4,6\ 2\ 2} \\ -\ 2,8\ 6\ 7 \\ \hline 5\ 5 \end{array}$$

11.

$$\begin{array}{r} 526 \\ -\ 87 \end{array}$$

$$\begin{array}{r} \$610 \\ -\ 75 \end{array}$$

$$\begin{array}{r} 263 \\ -\ 185 \end{array}$$

$$\begin{array}{r} 384 \\ -\ 196 \end{array}$$

$$\begin{array}{r} 451 \\ -\ 173 \end{array}$$

12.

$$\begin{array}{r} 2,475 \\ -\ 388 \end{array}$$

$$\begin{array}{r} 4,284 \\ -\ 1,196 \end{array}$$

$$\begin{array}{r} 1,427 \\ -\ 898 \end{array}$$

$$\begin{array}{r} \$3,821 \\ -\ 1,946 \end{array}$$

$$\begin{array}{r} 5,235 \\ -\ 2,789 \end{array}$$

13. You are a driver for McCarty Trucking Company. Complete the weekly mileage record shown below.
   a) For each day, subtract the "Odometer Begins" reading from the "Odometer Ends" reading. Write the difference in the "Daily Mileage" column.
   b) Add the completed "Daily Mileage" column to find the Weekly Total.

Example: 6/8

Od. Ends
$$\begin{array}{r} \overset{5\ 15}{9,6\ 5\ 9} \\ \end{array}$$
Od. Begins
$$\begin{array}{r} -\ 9,2\ 7\ 8 \\ \hline 3\ 8\ 1 \end{array}$$

Week of: June 8   **Name:**

Date	Odometer Begins	Odometer Ends	Daily Mileage
6/8	9,278	9,659	381
6/9	9,659	9,957	
6/10	9,957	10,348	
6/11	10,348	10,712	
6/12	10,712	11,097	
6/13	11,097	11,498	
6/14	11,498	11,850	
		Weekly Total	

Subtracting and Estimating

In daily life, estimating is your best way of quickly checking a math answer. The first step of estimating is to round numbers you are working with. Here are a couple of "rules of thumb" about the best way to round numbers:

- numbers between 10 and 99: round to the nearest ten

- numbers betwen 100 and 999: round to the nearest hundred

- numbers between 1,000 and 9,999: round to the nearest thousand

▼ MATH TIP

The "rules of thumb" shown at left are also known as rounding to the **lead digit**.

To round to the lead digit, you round to the place value of the first digit in a number.

▼ Practice

Circle the best estimate for the answer to problems 1–3.

1. Jason bought a jacket on sale for $59. If the original price had been $92, how much did Jason save?
   - **a)** $10
   - **b)** $20
   - **c)** $30
   - **d)** $40

2. When she left home, Stella was 916 miles from San Francisco. After driving 487 miles toward the city, how many miles is Stella from San Francisco?
   - **a)** 300
   - **b)** 400
   - **c)** 500
   - **d)** 600

3. Together, Jed's boat and trailer weigh 2,951 pounds. If the trailer alone weighs 378 pounds, how many pounds does the boat weigh?
   - **a)** 2,500
   - **b)** 2,600
   - **c)** 2,700
   - **d)** 2,800

4. A student worked the following subtraction problems with a calculator. Because of keying errors, the student got wrong answers on two of these problems.

   Estimate an answer for each problem. Then compare your estimate to the student's answer and decide which two problems the student solved incorrectly.

Problems	Student's Answers	Your Estimate
a) 86 − 39	47	_____
b) 692 − 319	643	_____
c) 8,207 − 5,853	2,354	_____
d) 9,068 − 4,885	5,183	_____

Subtracting from Zero

- To subtract from zero, borrow from the next column to the left.

The example shows how to borrow from the hundreds when there are no tens.

Example:

$$
\begin{array}{r}
607 \\
-\ 228 \\
\end{array}
$$

You can't borrow from 0, so you must first borrow 1 hundred from the 6 hundreds.

Step 1.

$$
\begin{array}{r}
5\ 10 \\
\cancel{6}\cancel{0}\ 7 \\
-\ 2\ 2\ 8 \\
\end{array}
$$

Write 5 in the hundreds column.

Add the borrowed 10 tens to the 0 in the tens column.

Step 2.

$$
\begin{array}{r}
9 \\
5\ \cancel{10}\ 17 \\
\cancel{6}\cancel{0}\cancel{7} \\
-\ 2\ 2\ 8 \\
\end{array}
$$

Borrow 1 ten from the 10.

Add the borrowed 10 ones to the 7 ones.

Step 3.

$$
\begin{array}{r}
9 \\
5\ \cancel{10}\ 17 \\
\cancel{6}\cancel{0}\cancel{7} \\
-\ 2\ 2\ 8 \\
\hline
3\ 7\ 9 \\
\end{array}
$$

Subtract each column:
- ones: $17 - 8 = 9$
- tens: $9 - 2 = 7$
- hundreds: $5 - 2 = 3$

▼ MATH TIP

Estimating can help you see if you are subtracting correctly.
- An estimate will tell you about what your exact answer should be.

Here's an estimate of the example at left:

Problem	Estimate
607	600
− 228	− 200
	400

▼ Practice

Find both an exact answer and an estimate for each problem below. Use the tip on page 77 to help you round.

Skill Builders

1.

$$
\begin{array}{r}
9 \\
3\ 10\ 12 \\
\cancel{4}\cancel{0}\cancel{2} \\
-\ 2\ 8\ 8 \\
\end{array}
$$

Estimate
$$
\begin{array}{r}
4\ 0\ 0 \\
-\ 3\ 0\ 0 \\
\end{array}
$$

$$
\begin{array}{r}
9 \\
7\ 10\ 14 \\
\cancel{8}\cancel{0}\cancel{4} \\
-\ 5\ 2\ 9 \\
\end{array}
$$

Estimate
$$
\begin{array}{r}
8\ 0\ 0 \\
-\ 5\ 0\ 0 \\
\end{array}
$$

$$
\begin{array}{r}
9 \\
2\ 10\ 15 \\
\cancel{3},\cancel{0}\cancel{5}\ 8 \\
-\ 1,\ 9\ 6\ 7 \\
\end{array}
$$

Estimate
$$
\begin{array}{r}
3,\ 0\ 0\ 0 \\
-\ 2,\ 0\ 0\ 0 \\
\end{array}
$$

2.

Estimate
$$
\begin{array}{r}
408 \\
-\ 219 \\
\end{array}
$$

Estimate
$$
\begin{array}{r}
503 \\
-\ 188 \\
\end{array}
$$

Estimate
$$
\begin{array}{r}
604 \\
-\ 308 \\
\end{array}
$$

3.

Estimate
$$
\begin{array}{r}
3,806 \\
-\ 1,189 \\
\end{array}
$$

Estimate
$$
\begin{array}{r}
5,105 \\
-\ 2,067 \\
\end{array}
$$

Estimate
$$
\begin{array}{r}
7,057 \\
-\ 4,392 \\
\end{array}
$$

Subtracting from a Row of Zeros

To subtract from a row of zeros, you borrow from the first nonzero digit to the left.

- All zeros in a row (except the 0 in the ones column) end up as nines.

Step 1.
```
    3  10
   A̸, 0̸ 0  0
 −  2, 3 7 1
```

Step 2.
```
        9
    3  1̸0  10
   A̸, 0̸  0̸  0
 −  2,  3  7  1
```

Step 3.
```
        9  9
    3  1̸0 1̸0  10
   A̸, 0̸  0̸  0̸
 −  2,  3  7  1
    1,  6  2  9
```

Compute both an exact answer and an estimate for each problem below. Use the tip on page 77 to help you round.

Skill Builders

4.
```
        9
    3  1̸0  10
   A̸  0̸  0̸          Estimate
 −     1  7  8      4 0 0
                  − 2 0 0
```

```
        9  9
    1  1̸0 1̸0  10
   2̸, 0̸  0̸  0̸       Estimate
 −     7  8  5     2, 0 0 0
                  −   8 0 0
```

```
        9  9
    5  1̸0 1̸0  10
   6̸, 0̸  0̸  0̸       Estimate
 −  2,  9  6  8    6, 0 0 0
                  − 3, 0 0 0
```

5.

	Estimate		Estimate		Estimate
300		400		1,000	
− 186		− 209		− 526	

6.

	Estimate		Estimate		Estimate
2,000		5,000		8,000	
− 839		− 2,482		− 5,285	

---

7. Best Buy Auto is having a Sunday Sale. Subtract to find the savings on each advertised item. Then compute an estimate as a check on your subtraction.

BEST BUY AUTO	Regular Price	−	Sunday's Price	=	Savings	Estimate
Car Accessories:						
a) Radio	$200	−	$129	=	_____	_____
b) Electric Windows	$400	−	$287	=	_____	_____
c) Air Conditioning	$600	−	$479	=	_____	_____
Automobiles:						
d) Sunset 2001	$9,000	−	$7,234	=	_____	_____
e) Flame 880	$8,000	−	$6,894	=	_____	_____
f) Browning TSX	$11,000	−	$9,107	=	_____	_____

SUPER SUNDAY SALE

Borrowing with Dollars and Cents

Borrowing from the Dimes Column

Example 1: Subtract $1.37 from $5.75.

Line up the decimal points and subtract.

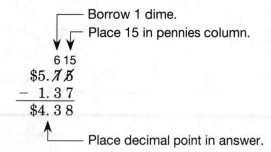

Borrow 1 dime.
Place 15 in pennies column.

```
    6 15
$5. 7̶ 5̶
 −  1. 3 7
$4. 3 8
```

Place decimal point in answer.

Borrowing across the Decimal Point

Borrow from the dollars column as if the decimal point weren't there. After subtracting, place the decimal point in the answer.

Example 2: Subtract $3.50 from $6.25.

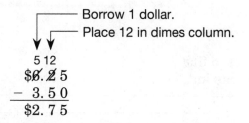

Borrow 1 dollar.
Place 12 in dimes column.

```
    5 12
$6̶. 2̶ 5
 −  3. 5 0
$2. 7 5
```

Example 3: Subtract 85¢ from $5.00.

Write 85¢ as $0.85.

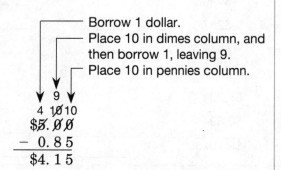

Borrow 1 dollar.
Place 10 in dimes column, and then borrow 1, leaving 9.
Place 10 in pennies column.

```
      9
   4 1̶0̶ 10
$5̶. 0̶ 0̶
 −  0. 8 5
$4. 1 5
```

▼ **Practice**

A. Subtract.

1. $2.46 $4.20
   − 1.29   − 2.18

2. $4.35 − $2.19   _____

3. $3.50 − $1.75   _____

4. $1.95 − $0.79   _____

5. $3.46 $6.40
   − 1.85   − 2.90

6. $6.25 − $5.90   _____

7. $12.45 − $6.70   _____

8. $5.75 − $0.93   _____

9. $1.50 − 80¢   _____

10. $3.00 − 47¢   _____

11. $2.00 − 89¢   _____

12. $5.00 − 76¢   _____

B. Estimate each customer's change. To estimate, round each amount to the nearest dollar. Then, compute the exact change.

1. Customer pays with a $5 bill for:

$3.89

Estimate: _____

Exact Change: _____

4. Customer pays with a $22.85 check for:

$7.24

Estimate: _____

Exact Change: _____

2. Customer pays with a $10 bill for:

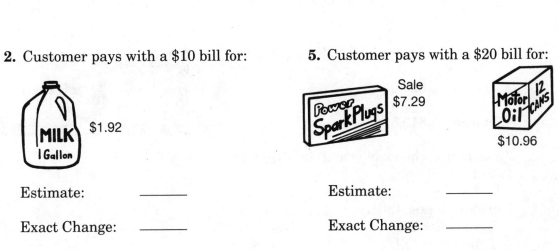

$1.92

Estimate: _____

Exact Change: _____

5. Customer pays with a $20 bill for:

Sale
$7.29

$10.96

Estimate: _____

Exact Change: _____

3. Customer pays with a $10 bill *and* a $20 bill for:

$7.98 and $19.89

Estimate: _____

Exact Change: _____

6. Customer pays with a $5 bill, a $10 bill, *and* a $20 bill for:

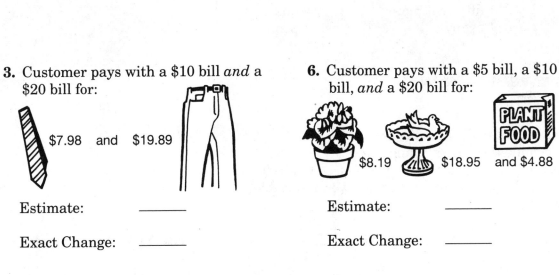

$8.19 $18.95 and $4.88

Estimate: _____

Exact Change: _____

ON THE JOB

Counting Correct Change

To **count change** correctly is an important skill. Clerks and cashiers need to be able to do it in a wide variety of jobs. Customers need to be able to do it to know they have received the correct change.

$7.49

Example: Marie pays for a $7.49 blouse with a twenty-dollar bill.
a) How much change should Marie receive?
b) What bills and coins should Marie be given?

To answer *a*, subtract $7.49 from $20.00.

$$\begin{array}{r} \$20.00 \\ -\ 7.49 \\ \hline \end{array}$$
Change: $12.51

To answer *b*, choose bills and coins that add to $12.51.

Here's one possibility:
1 ten-dollar bill
2 one-dollar bills
1 fifty-cent piece
1 penny

Here's another:
2 five-dollar bills
2 one-dollar bills
2 quarters
1 penny

▼ Practice

For each purchase described below,
a) determine the correct change, and
b) list the bills and coins that can be used to give this change. More than one correct answer is possible for each part *b*.

1. Customer pays with a $10 bill for:

 $3.89

Write Your Answers Here

a) Amount of Change:

b) Bills and Coins:

2. Customer pays with a $5 bill for:

 $1.26

a) Amount of Change: _____

b) Bills and Coins: _____

3. Customer pays with a $10 bill for:

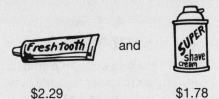

$2.29 $1.78

a) Amount of Change: _____

b) Bills and Coins: _____

4. Customer pays with a $20 bill for:

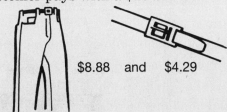

$8.88   and $4.29

a) Amount of Change: _____

b) Bills and Coins: _____

In each problem below, an incorrect amount of change has been given. Determine what the correct amount should be, and fill in each blank.

5. Customer pays with a $10 bill for:

 $3.41

Correct change: _____

Change received:

Change is too _____ by $_____ .
        (much, little)   **(amount)**

6. Customer pays with a $20 bill for:

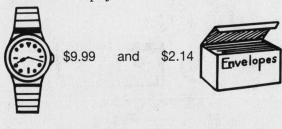

$9.99   and $2.14

Correct change: _____

Change received:

Change is too _____ by $_____ .
        (much, little)   **(amount)**

Figuring Change by "Counting Up"

Sometimes a clerk or cashier does not have a machine that tells how much change to give to a customer. In this case, the easiest way of making change is to "count up."

Sal Alvarez works at Downtown Hardware. Here's how Sal uses "counting up" to make correct change:

Suppose a customer buys a $6.89 hammer and pays with a ten-dollar bill. Instead of subtracting $6.89 from $10.00, Sal gives the customer change as he counts up from $6.89 to $10.00.

$6.89 plus **1 penny** makes $6.90
$6.90 plus **1 dime** makes $7.00
$7.00 plus **3 one-dollar bills** makes $10.00

Sal has given the correct change of $3.11: 1 penny, 1 dime, and 3 one-dollar bills. The customer is happy, and Sal feels great—he didn't need to subtract anything!

▼ **MATH TIP**

"Counting up" can also be used by a customer to make sure he or she is given the correct amount of change.

Customer's Change

▼ Practice

In each problem, determine what bills and coins can be given to make the correct change. More than one correct answer may be possible.

Number 1 is done as an example.

1. Emma buys a wrench for $11.68 and pays with a twenty-dollar bill.

   $11.68 + **2 pennies** makes $11.70
   $11.70 + **1 nickel** makes $11.75
   $11.75 + **1 quarter** makes $12.00
   $12.00 + **3 one-dollar bills** makes $15.00
   $15.00 + **1 five-dollar bill** makes $20.00

   Correct change: 2 pennies, 1 nickel, 1 quarter, 3 one-dollar bills, and 1 five-dollar bill.

Emma's Change

2. Brent places a fifty-cent piece on the counter to pay for a bolt that is priced at 8¢.

3. Placing a one-dollar bill on the counter, Jennifer wants to buy a 39¢ pack of gum.

4. Diane uses a five-dollar bill to pay for a $2.49 bottle of paint thinner.

5. Placing a ten-dollar bill on the counter, Manuel buys a yard rake that is priced at $4.39.

6. Monty buys a $6.25 screwdriver and pays with a twenty-dollar bill.

7. Patti pays for a $14.85 gallon of paint with a fifty-dollar bill.

IN YOUR LIFE

Balancing a Checkbook

Like most of his friends, Ty Billings has a checking account.
Carrying a checkbook is easier (and safer!) than carrying
cash. Ty pays most of his bills by check.

Ty is careful to keep a record of each transaction he makes:
writing checks, making cash withdrawals, and making deposits.

Ty keeps a record of these transactions in a check register—
a page of which is shown below. Although he is not charged
a fee for each check, Ty does pay a monthly bank service
charge of $8.50.

CHECK REGISTER
RECORD ALL CHARGES OR CREDITS THAT AFFECT YOUR ACCOUNT

NUMBER	DATE	DESCRIPTION OF TRANSACTION	PAYMENT/DEBIT (−)		✔T	FEE (IF ANY) (−)	DEPOSIT/CREDIT (+)		BALANCE $	
									675	00
310	5/1	Elm St. Apts.	$ 335	00		$	$		335	00
									340	00
311	5/4	Big Three Market	27	68						
	5/7	cash withdrawal at bank	40	00						
312	5/10	Northern Power Co.	108	39						
	5/16	payroll deposit					525	00		
313	5/17	Brennar's Furniture	82	50						

REMEMBER TO RECORD AUTOMATIC PAYMENTS/DEPOSITS ON DATE AUTHORIZED

When You Balance a Checkbook

- Subtract each check or cash withdrawal (Payment/ Debit column) from the Balance column.

- Add each deposit (Deposit/Credit column) to the Balance column.

▼ Practice

Balance Ty's checkbook.

1. Compute the daily balance in Ty's check register. Write each daily balance in the Balance column of the register.

   The beginning balance of $675.00 is shown, and the May 1 balance has been computed as an example:

   $$\begin{array}{r} \$675.00 \\ -335.00 \\ \hline \end{array}$$
   5/1 Balance: $340.00

2. After computing the May 17 balance, record the following new transactions in Ty's check register:
   a) Check 314, to Al's Auto on May 21 for $65.00
   b) Check 315, to Corner Market on May 22 for $21.50
   c) Check 316, VOID (torn up)
   d) Check 317, to New Hope Bank for $467.00 on May 27
   e) Cash withdrawal of $25.00 on May 28
   f) Payroll deposit of $525.00 on May 29
   g) Bank service charge of $8.50, to be recorded on May 30

3. Compute the daily balance in Ty's check register through May 30.

4. Ty bought a chair at Brennar's Furniture on May 17. The chair broke on May 23, and Ty took it back to be repaired. On May 31, Ty received a letter from Brennar's saying . . . "the chair is defective and cannot be fixed. Enclosed is your uncashed check for $82.50."
   a) How can Ty best record this information in his check register?
   b) What is Ty's actual balance on May 31?

▼ MATH TIP

Many people like to check a calculation right after it's made. In a checkbook you can do this by:
- doing each addition or subtraction twice
- checking addition with subtraction, and checking subtraction with addition.

Putting It All Together

Recording Transactions in a Savings Account

When you place money in a **savings account**, the bank
pays you **interest**.

- Interest is money that your money earns for you.

Typically, a bank will pay you 5 or 6 cents per year for each
dollar you have deposited in your savings account.

Imagine that the savings account record book (called a
passbook) below belongs to you.

PASSBOOK OF: _____				
		(your name)		
DATE	WITHDRAWALS	INTEREST	DEPOSITS	BALANCE
6/1				$341.82
6/2			$98.62	
6/23	$65.75			
6/30		$2.09		
7/3			$62.00	
7/9	$28.00			

▼ Practice

In this exercise, you will review what you have learned about adding and subtracting.

1. Compute the daily balance of your account.
   Remember: Add deposits and interest to the balance.
   Subtract withdrawals from the balance.

2. You forgot to record the following two transactions. Record these transactions and compute the new balance after each.
July 14: Deposit $145.00
July 28: Withdrawal $50.00

3. On July 29, you emptied your spare money jar and decided to put *all but $6.75* in your savings account. The money in your money jar is shown below:

a) How much money is in your jar?
b) How much money do you plan to deposit in your savings account?
c) Fill out the **savings account deposit slip** below.
   Currency refers to the total of bills—$1 bills, $5 bills, etc.
   Coin refers to the total of all coin money—pennies, nickels, dimes, etc.
   Total is the total deposit—the sum of currency and coin (and checks).

	CURRENCY		
CASH	COIN		
LIST CHECKS SINGLY			
TOTAL			

d) Enter this deposit in the passbook on page 88 and compute the new balance on July 29.

Multiplication

"Today I'll show you how to keep track of inventory, Henry. As the assistant manager, you'll be responsible for making sure our inventory doesn't fall too low. Take a look at this computer file."

Mr. Jackson, the office manager, pointed toward the computer screen showing the latest inventory log. He began to explain the different columns and rows.

Item	Number of Bags	Weight per Bag in Lb.	Estimated Number Used per Week
regular salt	210	40	70
rust-remover salt	50	40	75

The larger the inventory, the more helpful it is to use computers.

"I hope you've got a good handle on multiplication, Henry, because a lot of this work requires it. For example, how can you figure out how many pounds of regular salt are in stock now?"

"Well, I could look in the warehouse and count the number of bags, but I bet you're thinking of a quicker way," laughed Henry.

"You bet I am. You'll have more important things to do than counting inventory. When you need to get a count on a certain item, just call up the inventory log on the computer and look at the columns called 'Number of Bags' and 'Weight per Bag.' If you multiply together the numbers in those columns, you'll get your total."

"OK. So to find out the count on the regular salt bags, I'd multiply 210 by 40. I know a really fast way to do that—without using a calculator even."

"Terrific, Henry. Those are the kind of math skills that will really help us out here."

Think About It

- Suppose Mr. Jackson asked Henry to estimate how many pounds of regular salt were used in a <u>month</u>, instead of a week. What multiplication skills would he have to use?

How Does Multiplication Play a Part in *Your* Life?

As Henry learned, multiplying is really just a fast way of adding numbers. Think about your own life on the job and at home. Can you think of ways in which multiplication saves you time?

Have you ever gone to the grocery store and determined the cost of *several* of the same product just by looking at the price for a *single* item? Describe what you were buying and how you figured out the total cost.

_____

_____

Have you ever wanted to figure out how much you spend on heat, food, or car payments *per year* by looking at your *monthly* bills? How would you do this?

_____

_____

Do you think that some numbers are easier to multiply than others? What makes them easy to multiply?

_____

_____

Have you ever had a large amount of cash that you wanted to count up? Once you have sorted the twenty-dollar bills, the tens, the fives, and so forth, how would multiplication help you find the total amount?

_____

_____

Skills You Will Learn

Number Skills
- simple multiplying
- multiplying and carrying
- multiplying dollars and cents

Life and Workplace Skills
- ordering from a menu
- completing a purchase order
- shopping for discounts
- counting a large sum of money
- depositing receipts in a checking account

Thinking Skills
- making sure an answer makes sense
- estimating with dollars and cents

Calculator Skills
- multiplying whole numbers
- multiplying dollars and cents

Multiplying Single Digits

Multiplying is just a shortcut for adding.

Example: How many bottles are shown below?

Solution:

Adding: ____6____ + ____6____ + ____6____ = 18 bottles

Multiplying: ____3____ × ____6____ = 18 bottles

    number of   **bottles in**
    groups   **each group**

             ↑

            Product
            (the answer)

- The **times sign** (×) indicates multiplication.
  The answer is called the **product**.

▼ Practice

Write numbers for the following multiplications.

1.

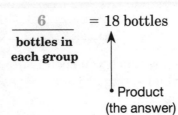

_____ × _____ = _____
 number of groups **dimes in each**   **dimes in all**
  of dimes   **group**

2.

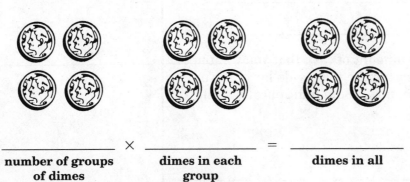

_____ × _____ = _____
 number of boxes **cans of juice**   **cans of juice**
 of orange juice **in each box**   **in all**

Basic Multiplication Facts

- A **basic multiplication fact** is the answer obtained when two digits are multiplied.

Examples: $3 \times 5 = 15$ $(5 + 5 + 5 = 15)$
$4 \times 6 = 24$ $(6 + 6 + 6 + 6 = 24)$

You use these facts in much of the problem solving that is required in school or at work.

▼ **MATH TIP**

Here are two special multiplication facts:
Any digit times 0 is 0.
Example: $5 \times 0 = 0$
Any digit times 1 is equal to that digit.
Example: $7 \times 1 = 7$

The Easy Way to Learn Multiplication Facts

Most books teach multiplication facts by having you memorize a multiplication table. That might be a hard way to learn. Here's an easier way.

- To learn multiplication facts, practice counting by 2s, 3s, 4s, and so on. The numbers you count will be the multiplication facts!

Examples:

Counting by 2s	Multiplication Facts
2	$1 \times 2 = 2$
4	$2 \times 2 = 4$
6	$3 \times 2 = 6$
8	$4 \times 2 = 8$
and so on	

Counting by 3s	Multiplication Facts
3	$1 \times 3 = 3$
6	$2 \times 3 = 6$
9	$3 \times 3 = 9$
12	$4 \times 3 = 12$
and so on	

1	2	3	4
2	4	6	8
3	6	9	12
4	8	12	16

Now notice how this "counting" method also works on a multiplication table. If you read across the row starting with 2 or down the column starting with 2, you are actually "counting by 2s."

▼ Practice

Practice counting by 2s, 3s, 4s, and 5s.
Practice until you can do each row without looking!

2s: 2, 4, 6, 8, 10, 12, 14, 16, 18
3s: 3, 6, 9, 12, 15, 18, 21, 24, 27
4s: 4, 8, 12, 16, 20, 24, 28, 32, 36
5s: 5, 10, 15, 20, 25, 30, 35, 40, 45

You know you're counting by 3s. When you reach 15, you can see that you counted five 3s.

▼ **MATH TIP**

When you count, you can keep track of the facts on your fingers.

Example: Count by 3s.

1	2	3	4	5
3	6	9	12	15

Now try counting by 2s, 3s, 4s, and 5s, and fill in each blank.
A few are filled in for you.

1. 2s: _____ , __4__ , _____ , _____ , _____ , _____ , _____ , _____ , _____

2. 3s: _____ , _____ , __9__ , _____ , _____ , _____ , _____ , _____ , _____

3. 4s: _____ , __8__ , _____ , _____ , _____ , _____ , _____ , _____ , _____

4. 5s: _____ , _____ , __15__ , _____ , _____ , _____ , _____ , _____ , _____

▼ **MATH TIP**

All multiples of 5 end in 5 or 0.

More about Counting

What if you can't remember a multiplication fact? Don't worry. Try counting up or down from a fact you do know.

Example: $5 \times 4 = ?$ You can't remember what five 4s are. But you do remember that four 4s (4×4) are 16. So, 5×4 is one more 4 than 16: $16 + 4 = 20$.

$$5 \times 4 = 20$$

Fill in the blank in each pair of facts below. In each pair, *think* of counting from one fact to the next.

5. $3 \times 5 = 15$ $4 \times 5 =$ _____
    three 5s   four 5s

11. $3 \times 2 = 6$ $4 \times 2 =$ _____
    three 2s   four 2s

6. $6 \times 3 = 18$ $7 \times 3 =$ _____
    six 3s   seven 3s

12. $8 \times 3 = 24$ $9 \times 3 =$ _____
    eight 3s   nine 3s

7. $6 \times 4 = 24$ $7 \times 4 =$ _____
    six 4s   seven 4s

13. $4 \times 2 = 8$ $5 \times 2 =$ _____
    four 2s   five 2s

8. $8 \times 5 = 40$ $9 \times 5 =$ _____
    eight 5s   nine 5s

14. $7 \times 4 = 28$ $8 \times 4=$ _____
    seven 4s   eight 4s

9. $8 \times 4 = 32$ $9 \times 4 =$ _____
    eight 4s   nine 4s

15. $7 \times 3 = 21$ $8 \times 3 =$ _____
    seven 3s   eight 3s

10. $8 \times 2 = 16$ $9 \times 2 =$ _____
    eight 2s   nine 2s

16. $6 \times 5 = 30$ $7 \times 5 =$ _____
    six 5s   seven 5s

Counting by 6s and 7s

Try counting by 6s and 7s. Practice, and then try to do them without looking.

6s: 6, 12, 18, 24, 30, 36, 42, 48, 54
7s: 7, 14, 21, 28, 35, 42, 49, 56, 63

▼ **MATH TIP**

Practice counting while you keep track on your fingers.

Now cover the rows above and fill in each blank below. Check with the rows above when you finish.

6s: __6__ , __12__ , ____ , ____ , ____ , ____ , ____ , ____ , ____

7s: __7__ , __14__ , ____ , ____ , ____ , ____ , ____ , ____ , ____

▼ Practice

Fill in the blank in each pair of facts below.
Think of counting from one fact to the next.

1. $5 \times 6 = 30$ $6 \times 6 =$ _____
 ⌐ five 6s   ⌐ six 6s

2. $3 \times 6 = 18$ $4 \times 6 =$ _____
 ⌐ three 6s   ⌐ four 6s

3. $2 \times 7 = 14$ $3 \times 7 =$ _____
 ⌐ two 7s   ⌐ three 7s

4. $8 \times 7 = 56$ $9 \times 7 =$ _____
 ⌐ eight 7s   ⌐ nine 7s

5. $6 \times 7 = 42$ $7 \times 7 =$ _____
 ⌐ six 7s   ⌐ seven 7s

6. $4 \times 7 = 28$ $5 \times 7 =$ _____
 ⌐ four 7s   ⌐ five 7s

7. $5 \times 7 = 35$ $6 \times 7 =$ _____
 ⌐ five 7s   ⌐ six 7s

8. $7 \times 6 = 42$ $8 \times 6 =$ _____
 ⌐ seven 6s   ⌐ eight 6s

Switch the order of multiplication facts.

9. $5 \times 4 = 20$ __4__ $\times$ __5__ = __20__

10. $7 \times 5 = 35$ ___ $\times$ ___ = ___

11. $6 \times 3 = 18$ ___ $\times$ ___ = ___

12. $7 \times 6 = 42$ ___ $\times$ ___ = ___

13. $7 \times 0 = 0$ ___ $\times$ ___ = ___

14. $5 \times 6 = 30$ ___ $\times$ ___ = ___

▼ **MATH TIP**

Switching the order in a multiplication problem doesn't change the answer.
 If you can't remember a fact, try switching the numbers.
Example: $6 \times 4 = 24$
$4 \times 6 = 24$

Counting by 8s and 9s

Now try counting by 8s and 9s. See if you can do them without looking at these rows:

8s: 8, 16, 24, 32, 40, 48, 56, 64, 72
9s: 9, 18, 27, 36, 45, 54, 63, 72, 81

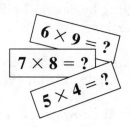

Now cover the rows above and fill in each blank below.

8s: __8__ , __16__ , ____ , ____ , ____ , ____ , ____ , ____ , ____

9s: __9__ , __18__ , ____ , ____ , ____ , ____ , ____ , ____ , ____

▼ Practice

Fill in the blank in each pair of facts below.
Think of counting from one fact to the next.

1. $5 \times 8 = 40$ $6 \times 8 =$ _____
    five 8s   six 8s

2. $7 \times 8 = 56$ $8 \times 8 =$ _____
    seven 8s   eight 8s

3. $8 \times 9 = 72$ $9 \times 9 =$ _____
    eight 9s   nine 9s

4. $6 \times 9 = 54$ $7 \times 9 =$ _____
    six 9s   seven 9s

5. $5 \times 9 = 45$ $6 \times 9 =$ _____
    five 9s   six 9s

6. $3 \times 9 = 27$ $4 \times 9=$ _____
    three 9s   four 9s

7. $3 \times 8 = 24$ $4 \times 8 =$ _____
    three 8s   four 8s

8. $2 \times 9 = 18$ $3 \times 9 =$ _____
    two 9s   three 9s

Switch the order of multiplication facts below.

9. $5 \times 8 = 40$ __8__ $\times$ __5__ $=$ __40__

10. $7 \times 9 = 63$ ___ $\times$ ___ $=$ ___

11. $8 \times 6 = 48$ ___ $\times$ ___ $=$ ___

12. $6 \times 9 = 54$ ___ $\times$ ___ $=$ ___

13. $4 \times 8 = 32$ ___ $\times$ ___ $=$ ___

14. $5 \times 9 = 45$ ___ $\times$ ___ $=$ ___

15. $7 \times 6 = 42$ ___ $\times$ ___ $=$ ___

FLASH CARDS

Many people find it helpful to use flash cards while learning multiplication facts.

Many bookstores have multiplication flash cards, or you can make your own if you wish to use them.

16. Build your own multiplication table by counting. Fill in the rows or columns below by using the multiplication facts you know. If you get stuck, count up or down from a fact you do know, or change the order of the numbers.

1	2	3	4	5	6	7	8	9	10
2									
3		9							
4			16						
5				25					
6					36				
7						49			
8							64		
9								81	
10									100

17. Below is the weekly work record of Manuel Garcia.
   a) Multiply to compute **Gross Pay per Day**.
   b) Add to determine Manuel's **Weekly Gross Pay**.

	Hours per Day	Pay per Hour	Gross Pay per Day
Monday	6	$6	_____
Tuesday	8	$6	_____
Wednesday	5	$6	_____
Thursday	9	$6	_____
Friday	7	$6	_____
Saturday	4	$9	_____
		Weekly Gross Pay:	_____

▼ **MATH TIP**

If you get stuck on a multiplication fact, try two strategies you've learned.
- Count up or down from a fact you do know.
- Switch the order of the problem. For example, if you can't remember 9×4, you may remember $4 \times 9 = 36$.

Multiplying by One Digit

To multiply a larger number by a one-digit number, multiply the top number one digit at a time.

- Multiply the ones.
- Multiply the tens.
- Multiply the hundreds, and so on.

Example:

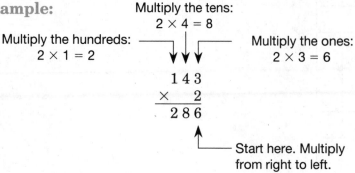

Start here. Multiply from right to left.

▼ **MATH TIP**

Write the product of the ones digit in the ones column, the product of the tens digit in the tens column, and so on.

▼ **Practice**

Multiply.

1.

32	12	21	$30	11	23¢
× 3	× 2	× 4	× 3	× 7	× 3
96					

2.

43	$61	70	54	81	$32
× 3	× 5	× 8	× 2	× 9	× 4
129					

  └ 3 × 4 = 12

3.

231	322	$411	213	324	230
× 3	× 2	× 2	× 3	× 2	× 3
693					

4.

632	812	511	721	$911	520
× 3	× 4	× 8	× 4	× 7	× 4
1,896					

  └ 3 × 6 = 18

In problems 5–7, circle your answer choice.

5. Rory makes a $91 car payment each month. How much does he spend in car payments each six months?

   a) $540
   b) $546
   c) $636

6. If dining room chairs are on sale for $112 each, how much does a group of 4 chairs cost?

   a) $448
   b) $488
   c) $492

7. On each load, Joanna carries 501 bricks to the construction site. How many total bricks can Joanna haul in 7 loads?

   a) 3,007
   b) 3,507
   c) 3,577

8. The Reynolds family is preparing a 3-month budget. They want to know how much they spend each 3 months on each of the items listed below.
   a) Multiply to find each **3-Month Total**.
   b) Add to find **Total 3-Month Expenses**.

Item	Average Monthly Cost				3-Month Total
Rent	$310	×	3	=	_____
Electricity	$ 32	×	3	=	_____
Gas	$ 62	×	3	=	_____
Car Payment	$210	×	3	=	_____
Insurance	$ 53	×	3	=	_____
Food	$310	×	3	=	_____
Telephone	$ 22	×	3	=	_____

Total 3-Month Expenses: _____

   c) The Reynoldses' total take-home monthly income is $1,320. How much do the Reynoldses take home each 3 months? _____

   d) After paying their Total 3-Month Expenses (computed in part *b* above), how much do the Reynoldses have left over each 3-month period? _____

FOCUS ON CALCULATORS

Multiplying

Multiplying Two Numbers

- The **multiply key** $\times$ is used to multiply two numbers.

Example 1: To multiply 37 by 8 on your calculator, press keys as shown at right.

Press Keys	Display Reads
C	0.
3 7	37.
×	37.
8	8.
=	296.

Answer: 296

Multiplying More Than Two Numbers

To multiply more than two numbers:

- Enter each number, and then press $\times$.

- Press $=$ only after entering the final number.

Example 2: At the Memorial Day Sale, how much will you pay for 3 cases of orange juice concentrate?

Memorial Day Sale

All Juice
Concentrate
$.79 per can

1 case

Press Keys	Display Reads
C	0.
. 7 9	0.79
×	0.79
2 4	24.
×	18.96
3	3.
=	56.88

To solve, multiply $.79 by the total number of cans—the number of cans per case (24) times the number of cases (3).

$.79 × 24 × 3

Answer: $56.88

▼ Practice

A. Fill in the key symbols to show how to calculate each answer.

Example: 23×14 〔C〕〔2〕〔3〕〔×〕〔1〕〔4〕〔=〕

1. 47×19 ⬭⬭⬭⬭⬭⬭⬭

2. $\$1.89 \times 7$ ⬭⬭⬭⬭⬭⬭⬭⬭

3. $9 \times 8 \times 7$ ⬭⬭⬭⬭⬭⬭⬭

4. $\$0.89 \times 12 \times 4$ ⬭⬭⬭⬭⬭⬭⬭⬭⬭⬭

— No need to enter a lone zero **before** the decimal point.

B. Solve these problems on your calculator.

1. 8×9 45×7 105×39

2. $9 \times 6 \times 4$ $14 \times 8 \times 6$ $123 \times 34 \times 9$

3. $\$1.29 \times 8 \times 6$ $\$2.84 \times 6 \times 2$ $\$5.50 \times 24 \times 5$

4. Picture yourself as an office manager. To compute the yearly costs of certain office supplies, you set up the chart shown below.
a) Multiply to find each Average Yearly Cost.
b) Add to find Total Yearly Costs.

Item	Average Cost of Each (A)		Average # Used Up Each Work Day (B)		Work Days per Year (C)		Average Yearly Cost (A × B × C)
1. Envelopes	$0.08	×	36	×	250	=	$720
2. Stamps	$0.25	×	36	×	250	=	
3. Pencils	$0.13	×	4	×	250	=	
4. Pens	$0.89	×	2	×	250	=	
5. Typing Paper	$0.02	×	74	×	250	=	
6. Phone Calls (long distance)	$3.00	×	3	×	250	=	

Total Yearly Costs:_____

Multiplying and Carrying

When the product of two digits is 10 or more, you must **carry**.

- Place the carried digit at the top of the column to the left.

- Then multiply, and add the carried digit.

▼ **MATH TIP**

Carrying is also called **renaming** or **regrouping**.

Example:
$$\begin{array}{r} 28 \\ \times\ 7 \\ \hline \end{array}$$

Step 1. Multiply the ones:
$7 \times 8 = 56$

Step 2. Multiply the tens:
$7 \times 2 = 14$

Add the carried 5:
$14 + 5 = 19$

Write 19 (14 + 5) in the tens and hundreds places.

$$\begin{array}{r} 5 \\ 28 \\ \times\quad 7 \\ \hline 196 \end{array}$$

Carry 5 to top of tens column.

Place 6 in ones place.

- Be sure to multiply the tens *before* adding the carried digit.

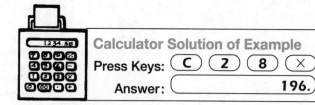

Calculator Solution of Example

Press Keys: C 2 8 × 7 =

Answer: 196.

▼ **Practice**

Multiply. Complete each row of partially worked Skill Builders. Then solve the following problems.

Carrying to the Tens Column

Skill Builders					
1. $\begin{array}{r}1\\14\\\times\ 4\\\hline 6\end{array}$	$\begin{array}{r}2\\28\\\times\ 3\\\hline 4\end{array}$	$\begin{array}{r}3\\47\\\times\ 5\\\hline 5\end{array}$	$\begin{array}{r}3\\118\\\times\ 4\\\hline 2\end{array}$	$\begin{array}{r}2\\227\\\times\ 3\\\hline 1\end{array}$	$\begin{array}{r}3\\416\\\times\ 6\\\hline 6\end{array}$

2. $\begin{array}{r}12¢\\\times\ 7\\\hline\end{array}$	$\begin{array}{r}16\\\times\ 3\\\hline\end{array}$	$\begin{array}{r}\$27\\\times\ 3\\\hline\end{array}$	$\begin{array}{r}37\\\times\ 4\\\hline\end{array}$	$\begin{array}{r}43\\\times\ 7\\\hline\end{array}$	$\begin{array}{r}52\\\times\ 9\\\hline\end{array}$

3. $\begin{array}{r}76\\\times\ 8\\\hline\end{array}$	$\begin{array}{r}\$49\\\times\ 6\\\hline\end{array}$	$\begin{array}{r}64\\\times\ 9\\\hline\end{array}$	$\begin{array}{r}116\\\times\ 6\\\hline\end{array}$	$\begin{array}{r}129\\\times\ 3\\\hline\end{array}$	$\begin{array}{r}\$214\\\times\ 5\\\hline\end{array}$

Being Careful with Zeros

Multiplying numbers with zeros can be tricky.
But you'll do fine if you remember these two rules:

- The product of any number times 0 is 0.

- Multiply the zero first, then add the carried digit.

Example:

$$\begin{array}{r} \overset{4}{}2\,0\,8 \\ \times\quad 6 \\ \hline 1,2\,4\,8 \end{array}$$

Step 1. $6 \times 8 = 48$ Write the 8, carry the 4.

Step 2. $6 \times 0 = 0$ Add the carried 4 to the 0.
$0 + 4 = 4$
Write 4 in the tens place.

Step 3. $6 \times 2 = 12$ Write the 12.

Skill Builders

4.

$\overset{2}{}2\,0\,9$	$\overset{4}{}1\,0\,6$	$\overset{3}{}3\,0\,7$	$\overset{5}{}5\,0\,6$	$\overset{4}{}4\,0\,5$
$\times\quad 3$	$\times\quad 8$	$\times\quad 5$	$\times\quad 9$	$\times\quad 8$
7	8	5	4	0

5.

108	206	305	$608	809
$\times\ 6$	$\times\ 4$	$\times\ 9$	$\times\ 8$	$\times\ 6$

Carrying to the Hundreds Column

Skill Builders

Example

6.

$\boxed{1}$ $1\,4\,3$	$\overset{1}{}2\,4\,2$	$\overset{2}{}3\,5\,0$	$\overset{4}{}2\,8\,1$	$\overset{4}{}6\,5\,0$
$\times\quad 3$	$\times\quad 4$	$\times\quad 5$	$\times\quad 6$	$\times\quad 8$
$4\,2\,9$	$6\,8$	$5\,0$	$8\,6$	$0\,0$

7.

152	163	$280	242	391
$\times\ 4$	$\times\ 3$	$\times\ 3$	$\times\ 4$	$\times\ 2$

8.

$362	783	571	$680	494
$\times\ 4$	$\times\ 3$	$\times\ 6$	$\times\ 8$	$\times\ 2$

Carrying to the Thousands Column

Example

9.
[1]	2	1	4	7
2,430	1,512	2,423	4,600	7,810
× 3	× 4	× 3	× 7	× 9
7,290	048	269	200	290

10.
3,420	$2,411	3,523	5,800	4,910
× 4	× 5	× 3	× 2	× 4

11.
4,811	3,900	5,400	$4,710	8,911
× 6	× 7	× 9	× 8	× 7

Circle your answer choice for problems 12–15.

12. Belinda bought nine 16-ounce containers of yogurt on sale. How many total ounces of yogurt did she buy?

   a) 114
   b) 134
   c) 144
   d) 164

13. Ferdy makes a $115 car payment each month. How much does he pay each 6 months?

   a) $660
   b) $690
   c) $760
   d) $790

14. On Saturday, Lucy sold 7 Eagle Recliners. If each recliner was on sale for $390, what total value of sales did Lucy make?

   a) $2,430
   b) $2,530
   c) $2,630
   d) $2,730

15. Mario makes 3 round-trip flights to San Francisco each year. If each trip covers a total of 5,912 miles, how many total miles does Mario fly each year?

   a) 17,736
   b) 17,836
   c) 17,936
   d) 18,036

16. As purchasing agent for Pete's Construction, you are in charge of ordering carpet for the new Industrial Arts Building. Complete the order form below.
  a) Multiply to find each total amount.
  b) Add to find the overall total.

Order Form				
Room Size (a)		Number of Rooms (b)		Total Amount for Each Group (a × b)
1. 45 sq. yd.*	×	8	=	360 sq. yd.
2. 60 sq. yd.	×	9	=	_____
3. 84 sq. yd.	×	7	=	_____
4. 124 sq. yd.	×	4	=	_____
5. 162 sq. yd.	×	3	=	_____
6. 192 sq. yd.	×	2	=	_____
			Total:	_____

* sq. yd. means square yards

17. You work in the shipping department of Auto Parts Wholesalers. You want to know how many cases of each listed item were shipped this week.

For each item, multiply to find the number of cases shipped.

Shipping Information				
Item	Cases per Truck (a)	Number of Truckloads (b)		Total Cases Shipped (a × b)
1. Oil	1,710	× 8	=	_____
2. Brake Fluid	2,600	× 9	=	_____
3. Antifreeze	1,923	× 3	=	_____
4. Grease	4,720	× 4	=	_____
5. Car Wax	5,910	× 6	=	_____

Carrying to Two or More Columns

Example:
```
   5 4
   3 9 7
×     6
───────
2, 3 8 2
```

Step 1.

Multiply the ones: 6 × 7 = 42
Carry 4 to the tens column.

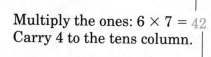

Carry 4 to the tens column.

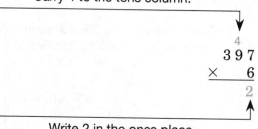

```
        4
      3 9 7
×         6
─────────
          2
```

Write 2 in the ones place.

Step 2.

Multiply the tens: 6 × 9 = 54
　Add the carried 4: 54 + 4 = 58
　Carry 5 to the hundreds
　column.

Carry 5 to the hundreds column.

```
      5 4
      3 9 7
×         6
─────────
        8 2
```

Write 8 in the tens place.

Step 3.

Multiply the hundreds: 6 × 3 = 18
　　Add the carried 5: 18 + 5 = 23

```
      5 4
      3 9 7
×         6
─────────
    2,3 8 2
```

Write 23 in the hundreds
and thousands places.

▼ Practice

Multiply. Complete the row of partially worked Skill Builders. Then solve the following problems.

Skill Builders

1. $\begin{array}{r} 1\,2 \\ 2\,5\,7 \\ \times \quad 3 \\ \hline 7\,1 \end{array}$	$\begin{array}{r} 2 \\ 3\,2\,6 \\ \times \quad 4 \\ \hline 4 \end{array}$	$\begin{array}{r} 3 \\ 7\,4\,6 \\ \times \quad 6 \\ \hline 6 \end{array}$	$\begin{array}{r} 2\ 4\,1 \\ 1,\,4\,7\,2 \\ \times \qquad 6 \\ \hline 8\,3\,2 \end{array}$	$\begin{array}{r} 6\,3 \\ 3,\,6\,8\,4 \\ \times \qquad 8 \\ \hline 7\,2 \end{array}$

2. $\begin{array}{r} 146 \\ \times \quad 3 \\ \hline \end{array}$	$\begin{array}{r} \$158 \\ \times \quad 2 \\ \hline \end{array}$	$\begin{array}{r} 245 \\ \times \quad 4 \\ \hline \end{array}$	$\begin{array}{r} 473 \\ \times \quad 6 \\ \hline \end{array}$	$\begin{array}{r} \$528 \\ \times \quad 8 \\ \hline \end{array}$

3. $\begin{array}{r} 1,425 \\ \times \quad 4 \\ \hline \end{array}$	$\begin{array}{r} 1,534 \\ \times \quad 3 \\ \hline \end{array}$	$\begin{array}{r} 3,593 \\ \times \quad 5 \\ \hline \end{array}$	$\begin{array}{r} \$4,294 \\ \times \quad 7 \\ \hline \end{array}$	$\begin{array}{r} 2,503 \\ \times \quad 6 \\ \hline \end{array}$

Being Sure an Answer Makes Sense

- After the last step in every problem, check your answer.

Ask yourself, "Does this answer make sense?"

When in doubt, **estimate**. An estimate gives you a number to check your answer against. If your answer is close to the estimate, you can be fairly sure you did your math correctly!

▼ **MATH TIP**

Estimating can often help you choose from among answer choices—even if the choices are not exact answers.

Example: Choose the most sensible answer.

There are 8 flights daily between Portland and Chicago. If each plane can carry 283 passengers, how many people can make this trip each day?

a) about 1,800
b) about 2,300
c) about 2,800
d) about 3,100

A quick estimate shows that choice *b* is the correct answer.

$$283 \longrightarrow 300$$
$$\times\ \ 8 \qquad \times\ \ 8$$
$$\overline{} \qquad \overline{2,400}$$

▼ Practice

Estimate an answer to each problem. Then, using your estimate as a guide, choose the most sensible answer from the choices given.

1. David George makes a $192 car payment each month. How much does he pay in 9 months?

   Estimate: _____

   a) about $1,200
   b) about $1,500
   c) about $1,800
   d) about $2,100

2. As a fast-food cook, Lilly is able to cook 1,136 hamburgers each day. At this rate, how many burgers can Lilly cook during her 5-day work shift?

   Estimate: _____

   a) between 3,000 and 4,500
   b) between 4,500 and 6,000
   c) between 6,000 and 7,500
   d) between 7,500 and 9,000

3. A truck is carrying 8 new pickups. If each pickup weighs 3,877 pounds, what total weight is the truck carrying?

   Estimate: _____

   a) about 20,000 pounds
   b) about 24,000 pounds
   c) about 28,000 pounds
   d) about 32,000 pounds

4. Together, Henry and his wife Estelle earn $28,940 each year. At this rate, how much will they earn in 7 years?

   Estimate: _____

   a) between $190,000 and $210,000
   b) between $220,000 and $240,000
   c) between $250,000 and $270,000
   d) between $280,000 and $300,000

Multiplying with Dollars and Cents

Example 1: Multiply: $4.83 × 5

Step 1. Place the numbers in a column. Multiply as you do with whole numbers.

```
      4 1
   $4. 83
   ×     5
   24  15
```

Step 2. $24.15

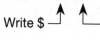
Write $ ⬆ ⬆ — Place decimal point to the left of dimes and pennies places.

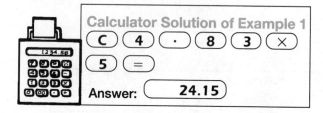

Calculator Solution of Example 1

(C) (4) (·) (8) (3) (×)
(5) (=)

Answer: (**24.15**)

Example 2: Multiply 78¢ by 6.

Step 1. Write 78¢ as $0.78.

Step 2. Write the numbers in a column, and multiply.

```
      4
   $0.78
   ×   6
   4 68
```

Step 3. $4.68

Write $ ⬆ ⬆ — Place the decimal point to separate dollars from cents.

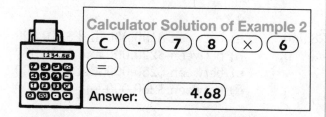

Calculator Solution of Example 2

(C) (·) (7) (8) (×) (6)
(=)

Answer: (**4.68**)

▼ **Practice**

Multiply.

1.
```
    $2.23          $3.13          $1.45
  ×    3         ×    4         ×    7
```

2. $6.75 × 5   _____

3. $9.85 × 4   _____

4. $14.50 × 8   _____

5. $38.99 × 3   _____

Write the answers to problems 6–11 as dollars and cents.

6. 61¢ × 3 $_____

7. 72¢ × 4 $_____

8. 49¢ × 5 $_____

9. 39¢ × 7 $_____

10. 75¢ × 8 $_____

11. 88¢ × 9 $_____

Estimating with Dollars and Cents

Estimate each purchase price below. Then, using your estimate as a guide, circle the letter of the exact purchase price from the choices given.

- To estimate, round each money amount to the nearest dollar before multiplying.

▼ **MATH TIP**

When your estimate is close to two answers, ask yourself, "Did I estimate higher or lower than the actual cost?"

1.

$1.12

a) $1.76
b) $2.16
c) $3.36
d) $4.86

Purchase: 3 loaves

Estimate: _____

5.

$1.89

a) $5.26
b) $7.56
c) $9.46
d) $11.26

Purchase: 4 gallons

Estimate: _____

2.

$0.89/pound

a) $7.12
b) $9.72
c) $13.22
d) $15.02

Purchase: 8 pounds

Estimate: _____

6.

$1.19

a) $7.41
b) $10.71
c) $14.51
d) $17.81

Purchase: 9 bags

Estimate: _____

3.

$12.45

a) $74.70
b) $78.90
c) $81.50
d) $87.20

Purchase: 6 boxes

Estimate: _____

7.

$4.89

a) $29.53
b) $31.83
c) $34.23
d) $39.13

Purchase: 7 calculators

Estimate: _____

4.

$9.69/gal

a) $42.65
b) $48.45
c) $52.35
d) $56.75

Purchase: 5 gallons

Estimate: _____

8.

$23.87

a) $190.96
b) $212.46
c) $235.76
d) $264.06

Purchase: 8 dictionaries

Estimate: _____

Ordering from a Menu

At some point in your life you have probably gone into a restaurant and ordered from a menu. What math skills do you use? Perhaps you **count** your money before you go in—just to make sure you have enough to buy something! Then, when you have decided what you would like to eat, perhaps you **add** to figure out how much your meal will cost. Or, do you just **estimate** the cost—to make sure you get the correct amount of change?

Have lunch now at Heavenly Burgers, and put your math skills to work!

HEAVENLY BURGERS

Sandwiches/Salads			Drinks		
				Sm.	Lg.
Heavenly Single	$ .99				
Cheeseburger	1.19		Soft Drinks	$ .59	$ .79
Heavenly Double	1.79		Milk	.60	.85
Double Cheeseburger	1.99		Coffee	.75	.95
Chicken Sandwich	2.14		Tea	.59	.79
Fish Sandwich	2.49		Hot Chocolate	.79	.99
Ham Sandwich	1.89				

	Sm.	Lg.	Desserts	
French Fries	$ .88	1.25	Pie	$1.39
Dinner Salad	1.29		Cake	1.29
Salad Bar		3.19	Ice Cream	.89

▼ Practice

1. You order the following items. How much will you have to pay?

   2 Cheeseburgers   _____

   1 Heavenly Double   _____

   3 Small Fries   _____

   1 Dinner Salad   _____

   3 Large Soft Drinks   _____

   1 Large Coffee   _____

         Total: _____

2. You and two friends have a certain amount of money. You want to order the following meal, and you want to quickly make sure you have enough money to cover the bill. Complete the cost estimate of this meal.

Estimated Cost

2 Heavenly Singles	$2 \times \$1.00 = \$2.00$
1 Chicken Sandwich	_____
3 Dinner Salads	_____
3 Small Fries	_____
3 Large Milks	_____
Total:	_____

3. Have you ever noticed that sometimes your estimate is *more* than the actual cost, and sometimes it is *less*? To see why, do the exercise below.

a) Compute both an estimate and exact cost for meals #1 and #2.

Meal #1	Estimate	Exact
3 Cheeseburgers	_____	_____
1 Large Fries	_____	_____
3 Pieces of Cake	_____	_____
3 Waters (free)		
Total:	_____	_____

Meal #2		
3 Heavenly Singles	_____	_____
3 Small Fries	_____	_____
3 Large Milks	_____	_____
Total:	_____	_____

b) For which meal is the estimate more than the exact price?

c) Why is one estimate more than the exact price while the other estimate is less?

▼ **MATH TIP**

- An estimated total will be less than an exact total when each estimate is less than each exact cost.
- An estimated total will be more than an exact total when each estimate is more than each exact cost.

Multiplying Numbers That End in Zero

Here is a shortcut for multiplying numbers that end in one or more zeros:

- Multiply the nonzero digits, and follow the product with the number of zeros in the two numbers.

Example 1: Lin made an average commission of $2,300 on each house she sold. If she sold 20 houses last year, how much did she earn?

Answer: $46,000

$$
\begin{array}{r}
\$2,300 \\
\times \quad 20 \\
\hline
\$46,000
\end{array}
\quad
\begin{array}{l}
2 \text{ zeros} \\
+\ 1 \text{ zero} \\
\hline
3 \text{ zeros}
\end{array}
$$

23×2

Example 2: Estimate the product 386 × 219.

To estimate, round each number to the nearest hundred, and multiply.

386 → 400   219 → 200

Answer: 80,000

$$
\begin{array}{r}
400 \\
\times \ 200 \\
\hline
80,000
\end{array}
\quad
\begin{array}{l}
2 \text{ zeros} \\
+\ 2 \text{ zeros} \\
\hline
4 \text{ zeros}
\end{array}
$$

4×2

▼ Practice

Multiply. Complete the row of partially worked Skill Builders. Then solve the following problems.

Skill Builders				
1. $\begin{array}{r}70\\ \times\ 30\\ \hline 21\end{array}$ add 2 zeros	$\begin{array}{r}60\\ \times\ 50\\ \hline 30\end{array}$	$\begin{array}{r}500\\ \times\ 30\\ \hline 15\end{array}$ add 3 zeros	$\begin{array}{r}700\\ \times\ 500\\ \hline 35\end{array}$	$\begin{array}{r}3,000\\ \times\ 600\\ \hline 18\end{array}$

2. $\begin{array}{r}50\\ \times\ 20\\ \hline\end{array}$ $\begin{array}{r}80\\ \times\ 40\\ \hline\end{array}$ $\begin{array}{r}\$90\\ \times\ 50\\ \hline\end{array}$ $\begin{array}{r}200\\ \times\ 40\\ \hline\end{array}$ $\begin{array}{r}\$400\\ \times\ 30\\ \hline\end{array}$

3. $\begin{array}{r}800\\ \times\ 50\\ \hline\end{array}$ $\begin{array}{r}7,000\\ \times\ 200\\ \hline\end{array}$ $\begin{array}{r}\$950\\ \times\ 700\\ \hline\end{array}$ $\begin{array}{r}\$4,000\\ \times\ 30\\ \hline\end{array}$ $\begin{array}{r}\$6,300\\ \times\ 30\\ \hline\end{array}$

4. Your boss wants a quick estimate of sales receipts from last year's sale of computer products. Complete each estimate below.

Item	Price	Number Sold	Estimated Receipts
a) Typing Programs	$78	29	$80 × 30 = $2,400
b) Business Programs	$91	47	_____
c) Education Programs	$88	32	_____
d) Computer Tables	$193	97	_____
e) Computers	$877	188	_____
f) Computer Manuals	$39	615	_____
g) Computer Paper (boxes)	$32	482	_____
		Total of Estimated Receipts:	_____

Multiplying by 10, 100, or 1,000

The shortcut gives us 3 easy rules to use when multiplying a number by 10, 100, or 1,000.

- To multiply by 10, put one 0 to the right of the number.

- To multiply by 100, put two 0s to the right of the number.

- To multiply by 1,000, put three 0s to the right of the number.

Example 1:

$$\begin{array}{r} 45 \\ \times\ 10 \\ \hline 450 \end{array}$$

Example 2:

$$\begin{array}{r} 156 \\ \times\ 100 \\ \hline 15{,}600 \end{array}$$

Example 3:

$$\begin{array}{r} 76 \\ \times\ 1{,}000 \\ \hline 76{,}000 \end{array}$$

5. Multiply to determine the number of each type of washer in a plumbing stockroom.

Washer	Number of Boxes		Number in Each Box		Total Number
#1	9	×	10	=	_____
#2	10	×	27	=	_____
#3	10	×	100	=	_____
#4	6	×	100	=	_____
#5	100	×	98	=	_____
#6	100	×	150	=	_____
#7	10	×	1,000	=	_____
#8	26	×	1,000	=	_____
#9	30	×	1,000	=	_____

▼ **MATH TIP**

Don't be confused by the order in which numbers are written. The answer is the same in either case.

Example:

23 × 100 = 2,300

and

100 × 23 = 2,300

Multiplying by Two Digits

When you multiply by a two-digit number, you multiply the top number by each digit of the bottom number.

The answer to each step is called a **partial product.**

- The answer to the problem is found by adding the partial products.

Example:

$$\begin{array}{r} 2\ 4\ 7 \\ \times\ \ 3\ 8 \end{array}$$

Step 1.

3 & 5 are carried digits

$$\begin{array}{r} 3\ 5 \\ 2\ 4\ 7 \\ \times\ \ 3\ 8 \\ \hline 1\ 9\ 7\ 6 \end{array}$$

Start the first partial product in the ones place. (247 × 8)

Step 2.

1 & 2 are carried digits

$$\begin{array}{r} 1\ 2 \\ 2\ 4\ 7 \\ \times\ \ 3\ 8 \\ \hline 1\ 9\ 7\ 6 \\ 7\ 4\ 1\ 0 \end{array}$$

← Write in place-holding zero.

Start the second partial product in the tens place. (247 × 3)

Step 3.

partial products $\left\{\begin{array}{r} 2\ 4\ 7 \\ \times\ \ 3\ 8 \\ \hline 1\ 9\ 7\ 6 \\ 7\ 4\ 1\ 0 \\ \hline 9{,}3\ 8\ 6 \end{array}\right.$

- Add the partial products.

▼ MATH TIP

Each partial product has its own carried digits. It is a good idea to write carried digits lightly in pencil. Then, you can erase them after you compute each partial product.

▼ MATH TIP

Some people like to use place-holding zeros to remind them where to start each partial product.

▼ Practice

Multiply. Complete the row of partially worked Skill Builders. Then solve the following problems.

Skill Builders

Write the 2nd partial product to the left of the place-holding zero.

1.

$$\begin{array}{r} 67 \\ \times\ \ 41 \\ \hline 67 \\ 2\ 68\underline{0} \end{array}$$

$$\begin{array}{r} 48 \\ \times\ \ 35 \\ \hline 240 \\ \underline{\quad\ 0} \end{array}$$

$$\begin{array}{r} 125 \\ \times\ \ 18 \\ \hline 1\ 000 \\ \underline{\quad\quad\ 0} \end{array}$$

$$\begin{array}{r} 258 \\ \times\ \ 74 \\ \hline 1\ 032 \\ \underline{\quad\quad\ 0} \end{array}$$

$$\begin{array}{r} 473 \\ \times\ \ 59 \\ \hline 4\ 257 \\ \underline{\quad\quad\ 0} \end{array}$$

2.

$22 × 17	43 × 24	59 × 16	$73 × 34	90 × 62

3.

147 × 48	375 × 53	$436 × 67	278 × 93	659 × 47

4. Carl is reviewing mileage figures for the trucks he uses in his business. He thinks that four of the Yearly Mileage figures (column *c*) are incorrect.

Use estimating to find these four incorrect numbers.

- Round each number in column *a* to the nearest 100.

- Round each number in column *b* to the nearest 10.

- Multiply.

Example: Truck M417 **Estimate:**

$$
\begin{array}{r}
583 \rightarrow 600 \\
\times\ 42 \rightarrow \times\ 40 \\
\hline
24{,}000
\end{array}
$$

The estimate of 24,000 indicates that the number 42,486 is incorrect.
(The correct mileage for truck M417 is 24,486.)

Truck#	Average Weekly Miles Driven (a)	Weeks Driven Each Year (b)	Yearly Mileage (c)	Estimated Yearly Mileage	Is Column (c) Incorrect?
M417	583	42	42,486	24,000	Yes
M675	688	47	52,336	_____	_____
M298	421	39	16,419	_____	_____
M318	592	52	43,784	_____	_____
M587	607	41	24,887	_____	_____
M638	717	32	22,944	_____	_____
M274	485	28	23,580	_____	_____

Shopping for Discounts

Like most shoppers, you are probably interested in getting the most for your money. Perhaps you know that this often means buying in quantity. Many stores give a discount when you buy several of the same item.

- To compute **total cost** on such a purchase, you multiply the number of items by the cost per item. Then subtract the discount if there is one.

Take a trip to 3 different hardware stores and find the lowest cost on a case (12 quarts) of Delux Car Oil.

Al's Automotive	Fred's Variety	Super Savers
Delux Car Oil	***Delux Car Oil***	***Delux Car Oil***
$1.18 per quart	$1.09 per quart	$1.14 per quart
$1.25 discount for case purchases	(no case discount)	"Buy 11, get 1 free!"

To find the lowest total cost, compute the case price at each store:

Al's Automotive	**Fred's Variety**	**Super Savers**
$1.18	$1.09	$1.14
× 12	× 12	× 11
2 36	2 18	1 14
11 8	10 9	11 4
$14.16	**$13.08 per case**	$12.54

Now subtract the discount.

(no discount given)

$12.54 for 11, and the 12th is free, so the case costs $12.54.

$14.16
− 1.25
$12.91 per case

$12.54 per case

You can probably see that Super Savers is the place to go for the best buy on Delux Car Oil.

1. Compute the price per case (12 bottles) of Skin Soft dish soap at each of the following three stores. Circle the best buy.

A & B Foods	Freddy's	Ervin's
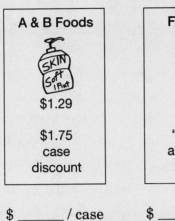		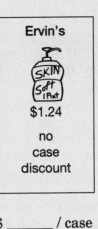
$1.29	$1.39	$1.24
$1.75 case discount	"Buy 11 and get 1 free!"	no case discount

$ _____ / case $ _____ / case $ _____ / case

2. Circle the store below that is offering the best buy on a purchase of 12 pounds of apples.

   Save More: $.98 per pound

   Home Foods: $1.01 per pound, and a $.50 discount on purchases of 10 pounds or more

   Shoppers Plus: $1.08 per pound, and a $1.50 rebate for purchases of $10.00 or more

3. At Value Hardware, the price of a quart of interior house paint is $4.95. The price of a case (12 quarts) is $48.99. How much of a discount is being offered for buying a case?

$4.95/quart
Case Discount

ON THE JOB

Completing a Purchase Order

As a stock supervisor at Kitchen Plus, one of your
responsibilities is to order items for the store as shelf
supplies run low.

To order new supplies, you need to fill out a **purchase
order form**. On this form, you list the items you are
ordering, the quantity of each item, and the wholesale
cost—the actual cost to Kitchen Plus.

You have started filling out the form below to order from
Valley Kitchen Supplies.

▼ Practice

Complete the Amount column for items 2–7, then compute
the Total Purchase amount. You can use your calculator.

Valley Kitchen Supplies

	Item #	Description	Quantity	Unit Price	Amount
1.	A1532	Sunshine Toaster	14	$8.25	$115.50
2.	C7729	Delux Waffle Iron	10	$17.95	
3.	G5379	Quigley Can Opener	15	$7.60	
4.	D4891	Super Dishwasher	4	$285.60	
5.	M3820	Summa Microwave Oven	7	$128.40	
6.	L2800	JJ Garbage Disposal	6	$86.50	
7.	R0085	Electric Frying Pan	17	$23.55	

8. | Total Purchase:

Note: To compute each amount, multiply the unit price
times the quantity. The unit price is the price for
each single described item.

Example: The amount you are spending on
Sunshine Toasters is computed by
multiplying $8.25 by 14.

$$\begin{array}{r} \$8.25 \\ \times\ \ \ 14 \\ \hline 33\ 00 \\ 82\ 5 \\ \hline \$115.50 \end{array}$$

Answer: $115.50

9. When the order arrived, there was a note saying that Valley Kitchen Supplies no longer carried Quigley Can Openers. Because this item wasn't shipped, what is the corrected Total Purchase Amount?

10. Several days later, your boss asks you to order the following additional supplies:

22 Super Sauce Pans, item # D8273, priced at $8.89 each
16 Electric Knives, item # E0938, priced at $14.99 each
9 Emerald Tea Pots, item # B2902, priced at $11.25 each
4 Electric Coffee Makers, item # Z1298, priced at $24.50 each

a) Write these items in the purchase order form below, filling in the Item #, Description, Quantity, and Unit Price columns.

b) Compute the total amount spent on each item, and enter these amounts in the Amount column. You can use your calculator.

c) Add the four amounts in the Amount column to find the Total Purchase amount. You can use your calculator.

Valley Kitchen Supplies

Item #	Description	Quantity	Unit Price	Amount
			Total Purchase:	

Multiplying by Three Digits

When you multiply by a three-digit number, you get three partial products.

- Start the first partial product in the ones column.

- Start the second partial product in the tens column.

- Start the third partial product in the hundreds column.

Example: Multiply
$$\begin{array}{r} 326 \\ \times\ 174 \end{array}$$

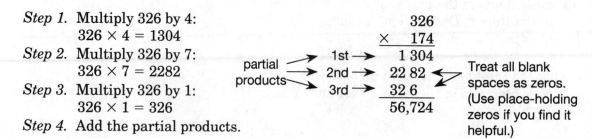

Step 1. Multiply 326 by 4:
$326 \times 4 = 1304$

Step 2. Multiply 326 by 7:
$326 \times 7 = 2282$

Step 3. Multiply 326 by 1:
$326 \times 1 = 326$

Step 4. Add the partial products.

```
          326
       ×  174
        1 304    ← 1st partial product
       22 82     ← 2nd
       32 6      ← 3rd
       56,724
```

partial products → 1st → 2nd → 3rd

Treat all blank spaces as zeros. (Use place-holding zeros if you find it helpful.)

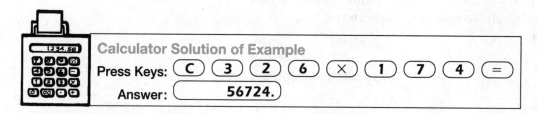

Calculator Solution of Example

Press Keys: (C) (3) (2) (6) (×) (1) (7) (4) (=)

Answer: (56724.)

▼ Practice

Multiply. Complete the row of partially worked Skill Builders. Then solve the following problems.

Skill Builders

Write the second and third partial products to the left of place-holding zeros.

1.
176	284	426	579	673
× 121	× 163	× 255	× 368	× 439
176	852	2 130	4 632	6 057
3 520	17 040	0	0	0
17 600	00	00	00	00

2.
$184	167	326	$365	584
× 113	× 122	× 213	× 244	× 469

3.

847	738	572	750	$906
× 481	× 344	× 418	× 521	× 562

4. Kerry is a bookkeeper for a wholesale business. He used a calculator to compute the Amount of Sales (column *c*) of several items sold over a 6-month period. Due to keying errors, Kerry computed incorrect answers for three of these items.

a) Use estimating to help identify the three incorrect sales amounts.

- Round each number in column *a* and column *b* to the nearest hundred.

- Multiply.

Example: Lawn mower   **Estimate:** $289 ⟶ $300
                              × 213 ⟶ × 200
                                        $60,000

The estimate of $60,000 indicates that the amount $61,577 is probably correct.

Item	Price (a)	Number Sold (b)	Amount of Sales (c)	Estimated Sales Amount
Lawn Mower	$289	213	$61,557	$60,000
Lawn Furniture	$185	527	$79,495	_____
Microwave Oven	$219	381	$53,439	_____
Dishwasher	$389	104	$40,456	_____
Kitchen Table	$321	94	$30,174	_____
Couch & Love Seat	$678	417	$282,726	_____
27-inch TV	$629	586	$258,594	_____

b) Compute correct amounts for each of the three incorrect sales amounts you identified above.

Shortcuts in Multiplication

In some multiplication problems, you can use a shortcut.

• You do not need to write a partial product that contains only 0s.

Example 1: Shortcut

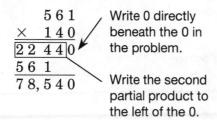

```
    5 6 1
×   1 4 0
2 2 4 4 0
  5 6 1
7 8, 5 4 0
```

Write 0 directly beneath the 0 in the problem.

Write the second partial product to the left of the 0.

Long Way

```
    5 6 1
×   1 4 0
    0 0 0
  2 2 4 4
  5 6 1
7 8, 5 4 0
```
← You do not need to write this partial product.

Example 2: Shortcut

```
    2 4 7
×   1 0 2
    4 9 4
2 4 7 0
2 5, 1 9 4
```

Write the third partial product to the left of the zero.

Write 0 directly beneath the 0 in the problem.

Long Way

```
    2 4 7
×   1 0 2
    4 9 4
    0 0 0
  2 4 7
2 5, 1 9 4
```
← You do not need to write this partial product.

Multiply.

1.
```
    173          $252
×    20          ×  30
```

2.
```
   $156          275
×   130          × 180
```

3.
```
    382          579
×   240          × 190
```

4.
```
    125          $157
×   103          × 106
```

5.
```
    283          $321
×   207          × 209
```

6.
```
    629          837
×   305          × 406
```

Multiplying Three Numbers

To multiply three numbers, pick any two and multiply them. Then, multiply the product of the two by the third number.

Example: Multiply $8 \times \$6.35 \times 21$

▼ MATH TIP

When multiplying two numbers, write the larger number as the top number.

Step 1.

$$
\begin{array}{r}
\$6.35 \\
\times\quad 8 \\
\hline
\$50.80
\end{array}
$$

Step 2.

$$
\begin{array}{r}
\$50.80 \\
\times\quad 21 \\
\hline
50\ 80 \\
1\ 016\ 0 \\
\hline
\$1,066.80
\end{array}
$$

Calculator Solution of Example

Press Keys: $(C)\ (6)\ (\cdot)\ (3)\ (5)\ (\times)\ (8)\ (\times)\ (2)\ (1)\ (=)$

Answer: 1066.8

▼ Practice

Multiply.

1. $9 \times 7 \times 6$ $13 \times 7 \times 8$ $\$1.25 \times 6 \times 4$

2. $35 \times 17 \times 8$ $\$1.68 \times 20 \times 9$ $\$7.50 \times 15 \times 8$

3. Determine the total purchase price of the quantity of each item ordered from Wholesale Food Distributors.

Wholesale Food Distributors Purchase Order

	Ordered Item	Price per Can (Jar)		Number in Each Case		Number of Cases		Total Price
a)	Corn	$0.79	×	24	×	5	=	$ _____
b)	Peas	$0.74	×	24	×	8	=	$ _____
c)	Catsup	$3.26	×	12	×	6	=	$ _____
d)	Mustard	$1.89	×	48	×	12	=	$ _____

ON THE JOB

Counting Money

Stores take in money every day. Counting these **cash receipts** is an important employee responsibility.

Example: Find the total cash receipts below.

Bills		Coins	
6	$20 bills	21	50¢ pieces
8	$10 bills	91	quarters
26	$5 bills	63	dimes
147	$1 bills	38	nickels
		27	pennies

▼ **MATH TIP**

To count total cash receipts:
* group like bills and like coins together
* compute separate totals for bills and coins
* combine the separate totals

Step 1. Compute the total of the bills.
* Multiply each group of like bills by the bill value.

Bills		Value
6	$20s	6 × $20 = $120
8	$10s	8 × $10 = $ 80
26	$5s	26 × $5 = $130
147	$1s	147 × $1 = $147
		Bill Total = $477

Step 2. Compute the total of the coins.
* Multiply each group of like coins by the coin value. Write each amount as dollars and cents.

Coins		Value in Dollars and Cents
21	50¢ pieces	21 × $0.50 = $10.50
91	quarters	91 × $0.25 = $22.75
63	dimes	63 × $0.10 = $ 6.30
38	nickels	38 × $0.05 = $ 1.90
27	pennies	27 × $0.01 = $ 0.27
		Coin Total = $41.72

Step 3. Combine the two totals.

Bill Total	$477.00
Coin Total	+ 41.72
Total Cash Receipts:	$518.72

1. Compute the total value of the bills below.

Bills	Multiply	Value
2 $50 bills	2 × $50	$100
8 $20 bills	8 × $20	_____
13 $10 bills	13 × $10	_____
19 $5 bills	19 × $5	_____
24 $1 bills	24 × $1	_____

Total Value: _____

2. Compute the total value of the coins below.

Coins	Multiply	Value in Dollars and Cents
7 50¢ pieces	7 × $0.50	$3.50
15 quarters	15 × $0.25	_____
37 dimes	37 × $0.10	_____
19 nickels	19 × $0.05	_____
11 pennies	11 × $0.01	_____

Total Value: _____

3. Lisa is a cashier at Tommy's Restaurant. On Friday night, Lisa was asked to count the cash receipts below and to fill in the form at right.

Count these cash receipts and enter the totals on the Cash Receipts Record.

Bills		Coins	
2	$50 bills	18	50¢ pieces
12	$20 bills	29	quarters
27	$10 bills	33	dimes
35	$5 bills	21	nickels
21	$1 bills	14	pennies

Cash Receipts Record

	Number	Total		Number	Total
$50	2	$ 100	50¢	_____	$_____
$20	_____	$_____	25¢	_____	$_____
$10	_____	$_____	10¢	_____	$_____
$5	_____	$_____	5¢	_____	$_____
$2	_____	$_____	1¢	_____	$_____
$1	_____	$_____			

Total Bills: $_____   Total Coins: $_____

Total Cash Receipts: $_____
(bills + coins)

Putting It All Together

Depositing Receipts in a Checking Account

Each Monday morning Wilma goes to the bank and deposits the weekend business receipts of Garcia's Furniture Store. These receipts consist of bills, coins, and checks. Her June 7 deposit is made up of the receipts shown below:

Bills	Coins	Checks
4 $50 bills	7 50¢ pieces	#13-36 $147.40
16 $20 bills	32 quarters	#26-21 $349.99
21 $10 bills	51 dimes	#33-06 $548.00
38 $5 bills	16 nickels	
19 $1 bills	28 pennies	

To make the deposit, Wilma used the **checking account deposit slip** shown below. She entered the totals of the bills and coins on the deposit slip:

Total Bills: $939.00   **Total Coins:** $17.68

Wilma then entered the value of each check. Next, she added to find the total.

Using the completed slip, she deposited the June 7 receipts.

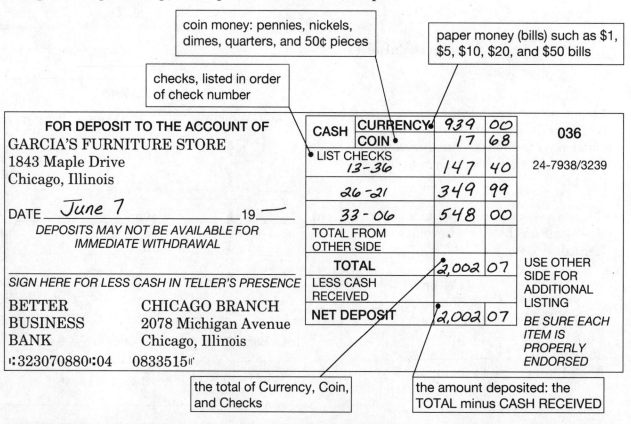

coin money: pennies, nickels, dimes, quarters, and 50¢ pieces

paper money (bills) such as $1, $5, $10, $20, and $50 bills

checks, listed in order of check number

FOR DEPOSIT TO THE ACCOUNT OF			
GARCIA'S FURNITURE STORE	CASH CURRENCY	939	00	036
1843 Maple Drive	COIN	17	68	
Chicago, Illinois	LIST CHECKS 13-36	147	40	24-7938/3239

DATE June 7 _____ 19 —

DEPOSITS MAY NOT BE AVAILABLE FOR IMMEDIATE WITHDRAWAL

26-21	349	99
33-06	548	00
TOTAL FROM OTHER SIDE		
TOTAL	2,002	07
LESS CASH RECEIVED		
NET DEPOSIT	2,002	07

SIGN HERE FOR LESS CASH IN TELLER'S PRESENCE

BETTER BUSINESS BANK

CHICAGO BRANCH
2078 Michigan Avenue
Chicago, Illinois

⑆323070880⑆04   0833515⑈

USE OTHER SIDE FOR ADDITIONAL LISTING

BE SURE EACH ITEM IS PROPERLY ENDORSED

the total of Currency, Coin, and Checks

the amount deposited: the TOTAL minus CASH RECEIVED

In this exercise, you will review what you have learned about multiplying whole numbers and decimals. On Monday, June 14, Wilma needs to deposit the receipts listed below.

Bills	**Coins**	**Checks**
2 $50 bills	4 50¢ pieces	#12-24 $125.00
9 $20 bills	20 quarters	#14-32 $300.00
12 $10 bills	45 dimes	#26-93 $225.00
40 $5 bills	15 nickels	
25 $1 bills	40 pennies	

1. a) Compute the total of the bills and coins:

Total Bills: $ _____

Total Coins: $ _____

b) Enter the total bills on the deposit slip below in the space labeled "CURRENCY."

c) Enter the total coins on the deposit slip below in the space labeled "COIN."

2. Enter the three checks on the deposit slip below in the spaces labeled "LIST CHECKS."

3. Add to find the total of currency, coin, and checks. Write this total on the line labeled "TOTAL."

4. Write the amount of the total on the line labeled "NET DEPOSIT."

FOR DEPOSIT TO THE ACCOUNT OF	CASH	CURRENCY		036
GARCIA'S FURNITURE STORE		COIN		
1843 Maple Drive	LIST CHECKS			24-7938/3239
Chicago, Illinois				
DATE _____ 19 ____				
DEPOSITS MAY NOT BE AVAILABLE FOR IMMEDIATE WITHDRAWAL	TOTAL FROM OTHER SIDE			
	TOTAL			USE OTHER SIDE FOR ADDITIONAL LISTING
_____ SIGN HERE FOR LESS CASH IN TELLER'S PRESENCE	LESS CASH RECEIVED			
BETTER CHICAGO BRANCH	**NET DEPOSIT**			*BE SURE EACH ITEM IS PROPERLY ENDORSED*
BUSINESS 2078 Michigan Avenue				
BANK Chicago, Illinois				
⑈323070880⑈04 0833515⑈'				

Division

"You're asking me to make decisions about things I can't predict, Celia. How do I know how much money I'll be bringing home next month? My paycheck is different every week. And how can I know how much I'll spend on food and other things? You know how prices are!"

Celia was trying to help her friend Tina come up with a budget that would allow her to put aside some money each month for savings. Tina had been complaining that "the money just flew out of her purse."

"You aren't listening to me, Tina. I asked you *about* how much money you think you'll make and *about* how much you'll spend each week. Of course some weeks will be higher and some lower. To budget your money, you just need to know the *average*."

"Average? I learned about averages in math class, but I never thought I'd use them," responded Tina.

"Well, I hope you learned something about division in that math class, because my

calculator is at home, and you need to know how to divide in order to find averages. Now let's add up this month's grocery receipts and divide by four to find out your *average* weekly food bill."

Budgets help you plan your spending and savings.

Think About It

- Why does Celia say to divide by <u>four</u>? (Hint: How many weeks are in a month?)

- Tina added up all of her monthly heating bills for the past year and wanted to find her <u>monthly</u> average. What would she have to divide by?

How Does Division Play a Part in *Your* Life?

Think about division as splitting up a whole amount into smaller amounts all of the same size. When do you do this in your everyday life? Have you ever tried to budget your money in the way that Tina is trying to?

How much time do you spend sleeping each night, on average? If you are like a lot of people, you sleep more hours on the weekend than on weekdays. Add up the hours you slept each night last week, then divide by seven to find the <u>average</u>.

_____

Have you ever had to <u>divide</u> numbers on your job? Describe the situation and tell whether you used a pencil, a calculator, or just your head.

_____

Have you ever tried to figure out how many miles your car can travel on one gallon of gas? How did you do it?

_____

Have you ever used division to figure out how much money you are spending on <u>one</u> item when you have the price for <u>several</u> of the items? Describe the situation.

_____

Skills You Will Learn

Number Skills
- division facts
- remainders
- dividing by one- and two-digit numbers
- dividing dollars and cents

Life and Workplace Skills
- finding an average
- making business decisions
- computing the lowest unit price
- estimating on the job
- keeping a mileage record
- using the distance formula
- working with a budget

Thinking Skills
- dividing and estimating
- deciding what to do with a remainder

Calculator Skills
- dividing whole numbers
- dividing dollars and cents
- working with remainders
- checking calculator answers

Dividing

To divide is to find out how many equal parts are in a group.

Example: If the bunch of 20 apples shown below is divided into 4 equal-size groups, how many apples will be in each group?

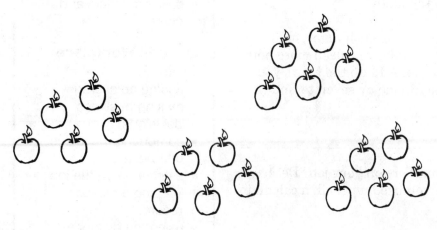

Solution: ___20___ ÷ ___4___ = 5 apples in each group

total number of apples   number of groups   ↑ each group

• Quotient (the answer)

• The *division sign* ÷ indicates division.
  The answer is called the *quotient*.

▼ Practice

Write numbers for the following divisions.

1.

_____ ÷ _____ = _____

total number of pennies   number of groups   pennies in each group

2.

_____ ÷ _____ = _____

total number of buttons   number of groups   buttons in each group

▶ 130

Basic Division Facts

Basic division facts come from the basic multiplication facts that you have learned. In fact, you can think of dividing as "undoing" multiplication.

To Solve:	You Think:	In Words:	Answer:
$9\overline{)36}$	$9 \times \rule{2em}{0.4pt} = 36$	9 times *what number* equals 36?	4
$63 \div 7$	$7 \times \rule{2em}{0.4pt} = 63$	7 times *what number* equals 63?	9

Write each answer on the line provided.

	To Solve:	You Think:	To Solve:	You Think:
3.	$4\overline{)12}$	$4 \times \underline{\ 3\ } = 12$	$6\overline{)18}$	$6 \times \rule{2em}{0.4pt} = 18$
4.	$3\overline{)27}$	$3 \times \rule{2em}{0.4pt} = 27$	$8\overline{)56}$	$8 \times \rule{2em}{0.4pt} = 56$
5.	$5\overline{)40}$	$5 \times \rule{2em}{0.4pt} = 40$	$5\overline{)20}$	$5 \times \rule{2em}{0.4pt} = 20$
6.	$9\overline{)54}$	$9 \times \rule{2em}{0.4pt} = 54$	$8\overline{)72}$	$8 \times \rule{2em}{0.4pt} = 72$
7.	$9\overline{)81}$	$9 \times \rule{2em}{0.4pt} = 81$	$8\overline{)64}$	$8 \times \rule{2em}{0.4pt} = 64$
8.	$36 \div 9$	$9 \times \rule{2em}{0.4pt} = 36$	$48 \div 8$	$8 \times \rule{2em}{0.4pt} = 48$
9.	$56 \div 7$	$7 \times \rule{2em}{0.4pt} = 56$	$42 \div 6$	$6 \times \rule{2em}{0.4pt} = 42$
10.	$48 \div 8$	$8 \times \rule{2em}{0.4pt} = 48$	$63 \div 9$	$9 \times \rule{2em}{0.4pt} = 63$
11.	$32 \div 4$	$4 \times \rule{2em}{0.4pt} = 32$	$72 \div 9$	$9 \times \rule{2em}{0.4pt} = 72$
12.	$56 \div 8$	$8 \times \rule{2em}{0.4pt} = 56$	$81 \div 9$	$9 \times \rule{2em}{0.4pt} = 81$

Using Counting with Basic Division Facts

If you don't remember a needed multiplication fact, you can use your counting skills.

* Think of dividing as asking, "How many of one number are there in a second number?"

Example: $6\overline{)42}$ asks, "How many 6s are in 42?"

Counting by 6s we find:

6, 12, 18, 24, 30, 36, $\boxed{42}$

— seven 6s

There are seven 6s in 42.

Try counting to solve each problem below.
Write each answer on the line provided.

	To Solve:	**You Count:**	**Answer:**
13.	$8\overline{)32}$	By 8s: 8, 16, 24, $\boxed{32}$	_4_
		— four 8s	
14.	$4\overline{)24}$	By 4s:	___
15.	$7\overline{)42}$	By 7s:	___
16.	$6\overline{)30}$	By 6s:	___
17.	$27 \div 3$	By 3s:	___
18.	$45 \div 9$	By 9s:	___
19.	$72 \div 8$	By 8s:	___
20.	$40 \div 5$	By 5s:	___

Math Facts

* The number being divided is always called the *dividend*.
* The number being divided by is always called the *divisor*.

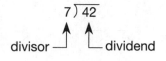

divisor — 　 — dividend

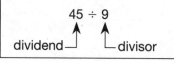

dividend — 　 — divisor

▼ **MATH TIP**

When written with a ÷ sign, a division problem such as 27 ÷ 3 asks, "How many 3s are in 27?"

Using either method, divide.

Write 4 in the ones place above the 6.

Example: $4\overline{)16}$ 4

21. $4\overline{)28}$ $3\overline{)18}$ $5\overline{)30}$ $4\overline{)36}$ $2\overline{)16}$

22. $5\overline{)15}$ $6\overline{)42}$ $9\overline{)27}$ $8\overline{)24}$ $7\overline{)35}$

23. $4\overline{)36}$ $5\overline{)45}$ $7\overline{)56}$ $9\overline{)63}$ $8\overline{)72}$

24. $8\overline{)64}$ $3\overline{)21}$ $7\overline{)49}$ $8\overline{)48}$ $6\overline{)36}$

25. $2\overline{)18}$ $3\overline{)24}$ $6\overline{)24}$ $9\overline{)81}$ $8\overline{)64}$

In problems 26–30, circle your answer choice.

26. Danny divided a box of 27 crayons among his three children. To be fair, how many crayons did he give each child?
   a) 7   **b)** 8   **c)** 9

27. Lynn sold $42 worth of coffee mugs at the community store. At $7 per mug, how many mugs did Lynn sell?
   a) 6   **b)** 7   **c)** 8

28. Three neighbors split the cost of a case of dish soap. If the case contains 24 bottles, how many bottles will each neighbor get?
   a) 7   **b)** 8   **c)** 9

29. Mrs. Pratt paid $72 for 9 books for her garden club members. In order to break even, how much should she charge each member for a book?
   a) $7   **b)** $8   **c)** $9

30. Five friends went out to dinner. The bill, including tip, was $45. If they split the bill evenly, how much did each pay?
   a) $7   **b)** $8   **c)** $9

Remainders in Division

A **remainder** is a number left over.

Suppose you bought 9 notepads for your office. You divided the notepads among the 4 secretaries. Each secretary got 2, and there was 1 notepad left over.

Using the letter *r* to stand for remainder, you would write this as

$$9 \div 4 = 2 \text{ r } 1$$

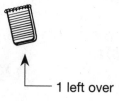

└─ 1 left over

Example: You also bought 31 pencils and handed them out to your 4 secretaries. How many did each secretary get?

Step 1. Ask, "How many 4s are in 31?"

☐   6   yes, $6 \times 4 = 24$

☑   7   yes, $7 \times 4 = 28$

☐   8   no, $8 \times 4 = 32$

$$4\overline{)31} \quad \begin{array}{r} 7 \\ \end{array}$$

Step 2. Multiply: $7 \times 4 = 28$.
Write 28 below 31.

compare

$$\begin{array}{r} 7 \text{ r } 3 \\ 4\overline{)31} \\ -28 \\ \hline 3 \end{array}$$

Step 3. Subtract: $31 - 28 = 3$

To be correct, the remainder must be smaller than the divisor: 3 is smaller than 4.

Answer: Each secretary got 7 pencils.
Three pencils are left over.

▼ **MATH TIP**

To check a problem with a remainder, multiply and then add the remainder.

Here's how to check the example:

multiply   then   add

$$\begin{array}{r} 7 \\ \times \ 4 \\ \hline 28 \end{array} \qquad \begin{array}{r} 28 \\ + \ 3 \text{ remainder} \\ \hline 31 \ \checkmark \end{array}$$

▼ **Practice**

Divide, and then check. Complete the row of partially worked Skill Builders. Then solve the following problems.

Skill Builders

1. $\begin{array}{r} 1\text{r} \\ 5\overline{)8} \\ -5 \\ \hline 3 \end{array}$ $\begin{array}{r} 1\text{r} \\ 7\overline{)9} \\ -7 \\ \hline 2 \end{array}$ $\begin{array}{r} 2 \\ 6\overline{)14} \\ -12 \\ \hline \end{array}$ $\begin{array}{r} 5 \\ 5\overline{)27} \\ \end{array}$ $\begin{array}{r} 8 \\ 6\overline{)52} \\ \end{array}$

2. $2\overline{)5}$ $5\overline{)9}$ $3\overline{)8}$ $4\overline{)9}$ $6\overline{)8}$

Deciding What to Do with a Remainder

As you found out, dividing often results in a remainder.
When this happens, you must decide what to do with the
leftover amount. Sometimes you:

- **Use the Remainder** (round up)

Patti can carry 2 gallons of punch in
each shopping bag. How many bags
will she need to carry 7 gallons to
the school picnic?

$$
\begin{array}{r}
3\ r\ 1 \\
2\overline{)\ 7} \\
-6 \\
\hline
1
\end{array}
$$

Answer: 4 bags

You **round up** to the next number
because Patti needs an extra bag to
carry the remainder (the 7th gallon).

- **Don't Use the Remainder** (round down)

Ben is making 3-foot long shelves. How
many shelves can he cut from a board that
is 8 feet long?

$$
\begin{array}{r}
2\ r\ 2 \\
3\overline{)\ 8} \\
-6 \\
\hline
2
\end{array}
$$

Answer: 2 shelves

You **round down** (drop the remainder)
because Ben can't make another shelf
from the leftover 2-foot-long piece.

▼ Practice

Divide, and decide what to do with the remainder as you
answer each question below.

1. After his daughter's birthday party, Dennis
   is taking Lara and her 18 guests swimming.
   If he can carry 5 kids in each trip, how
   many trips will he make to get them there?

2. On the average, it takes Karin 9 minutes to
   check a charge-card application form. How
   many customers can Karin help during her
   final hour of work?
   (1 hour = 60 minutes)

3. Jan is making skirts for her daughters.
   Each skirt takes 4 feet of material. If she
   has 18 feet of material in all, how many
   skirts can Jan make?

4. Part of Frank's job is to ship records in
   response to a customer's order. Packing
   6 records in each box, how many boxes
   will Frank need when mailing an order
   of 34 records?

FOCUS ON CALCULATORS

Dividing

To divide on a calculator:

- Enter the **dividend,** and press ⟨÷⟩.

- Enter the divisor, and press ⟨=⟩.

$$38\overline{)646}$$

divisor ——⬈   ⬉—— dividend

Example: Divide:

$$\$25.62 \div 6$$

dividend ——⬈   ⬉—— divisor

▼ **MATH TIP**

Remember that the number you are dividing *by* (divisor) must come **after** the ÷.

To solve, press keys as shown at right.

Answer: $4.27

Press Keys	Display Reads
C	0.
2 5 · 6 2	25.62
÷	25.62
6	6.
=	4.27

Calculator Discovery

Once in a while, you may accidentally try to do a calculation that your calculator is unable to do. The calculator will then display an *error symbol*—an *E* on most calculators.

- **Overflow error:** Multiplying numbers that give a product too large for the display. Example: 21,400 × 7,850

  1.6799000ᴇ

- **Division by 0 error:** Trying to divide by 0. You cannot divide by 0. Example: 36 ÷ 0

  0.ᴇ

If an error symbol appears on your calculator, simply press the **clear** key and redo your calculation.

▼ Practice

Identify the dividend and divisor in each problem. Fill in the key symbols to show how to solve each problem on a calculator.

1. 377 ÷ 13 =   dividend _____

divisor _____

2. 6)$7.98   dividend _____

divisor _____

⟨ ⟩⟨ ⟩⟨ ⟩⟨ ⟩⟨ ⟩⟨ ⟩⟨ ⟩   ⟨ ⟩⟨ ⟩⟨ ⟩⟨ ⟩⟨ ⟩⟨ ⟩⟨ ⟩⟨ ⟩

Divide as indicated.

3. $9\overline{)342}$ $\overset{\displaystyle\wedge}{\underset{\text{dividend}}{}}$

$13\overline{)273}$

$6\overline{)\$27.18}$

▼ **MATH TIP**

No matter how a problem is set up, always enter the number being divided (the dividend) into the calculator first.

4. $15\overline{)480}$

$24\overline{)816}$

$13\overline{)\$112.58}$

5. $136 \div 8 =$ $\overset{\displaystyle\wedge}{\underset{\text{dividend}}{}}$

$425 \div 17 =$

$\$21.14 \div 14 =$

6. $546 \div 14 =$

$910 \div 26 =$

$\$150.28 \div 26 =$

7. Rachel's inventory report needs to be finished. She knows the total number of items and their total cost. She needs to compute the cost per item (cost of 1 item).

Use your calculator to find the cost per item. Item 1 is done as an example.

Cost of 1 hairbrush: $\$19.56 \div 4$

Press Keys: (C) (1) (9) (·) (5) (6) (÷) (4) (=)
Answer: (4.89)

	Item	Number of Items	Total Cost	Cost per Item
a)	Hairbrushes	4	$19.56	$4.89
b)	Manicure Sets	7	$61.46	
c)	Hair Nets	12	$15.48	
d)	Nail Polish (bottles)	16	$44.64	
e)	Make-up Kits	23	$330.05	
f)	Perfume (bottles)	35	$437.15	

Calculators and Remainders

Look again at the following example:

You bought 9 notepads for the office. You divided the notepads among the 4 secretaries. Each secretary got 2, and there was 1 notepad left over.

or, $9 \div 4 = 2\ r\ 1$

Suppose we solve this same problem using a calculator.

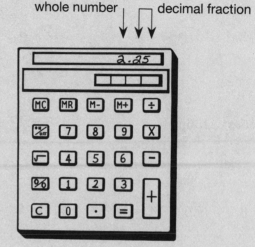

Press Keys	Display Reads
C	0.
9	9.
÷	9.
4	4.
=	2.25

The answer 2.25 contains both a **whole number part (2)** and a **decimal fraction part (.25)**.

• Your calculator displays a remainder as a decimal fraction.

Would you say that each secretary received 2.25 notepads? Of course not! The remainder, or decimal fraction, is not used in solving this problem. Now read the following example, and then do the problems on remainders. For these problems, you do not need to know about decimals. You'll learn about decimals in *Math Skills That Work, Book Two*.

Example:

Lee has a 137-foot-long piece of rope that she wants to cut into 11-foot lengths. How many 11-foot-long pieces can she cut?

To solve, divide 137 by 11.

As shown, Lee can get 12 pieces, each 11 feet long. The remaining piece is of no use to her.

Answer: Twelve 11-foot pieces

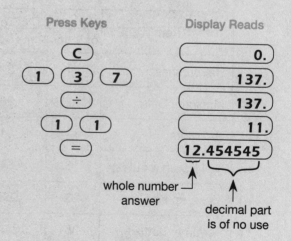

Press Keys	Display Reads
C	0.
1 3 7	137.
÷	137.
1 1	11.
=	12.454545

▼ Practice

In problems 1 and 2, circle your answer choice.

1. Norland Bus Company has been hired to take 419 students to a music concert. If each bus holds a maximum of 44 students, how many buses will be needed?

   a) 8
   b) 9
   c) 10

2. The elevator in Blaine's Sport Shop can safely lift 1,800 pounds. How many players of the Bulldogs football team can safely ride at one time if each player weighs close to 250 pounds?

   a) 7
   b) 8
   c) 9

3. Barry has been hired to move rock, fill dirt, and topsoil to a construction site. He is able to carry 12 cubic yards in his truck on each trip.

   Fill in the chart below to show how many trips it will take Barry to complete this job.

Material	Cubic Yards to Move	Cubic Yards Each Trip	Number of Trips
Rock	1,415	12	_____
Fill Dirt	2,910	12	_____
Topsoil	375	12	_____

   TOTAL NUMBER OF TRIPS: _____

4. Naomi wants to check her answers on a practice employment math test. She will use a calculator to check the whole number part of each quotient below.

   Using your calculator, find and then circle the three incorrect answers.

   a) $287 \div 9 = 33 \text{ r } 4$

   b) $748 \div 16 = 46 \text{ r } 12$

   c) $1,455 \div 7 = 207 \text{ r } 6$

   d) $4,526 \div 24 = 178 \text{ r } 3$

   e) $8,700 \div 40 = 217 \text{ r } 20$

   f) $9,462 \div 134 = 76 \text{ r } 51$

▼ MATH TIP

If the whole number part of the calculator answer and Naomi's answer are the same, Naomi can be confident that she worked the problem correctly.

Dividing by One Digit

Dividing is a 5-step process that combines many of the skills you now have.

For longer problems, you may need to repeat these steps more than one time.

5 STEPS OF DIVISION

- Divide, and write a digit in the answer.
- Multiply.
- Subtract.
- Compare.
- Bring down the next digit.

Example 1: Divide: $4\overline{)92}$

Step 1. Divide 4 into 9.
Write 2 over the 9.

Step 2. Multiply: $2 \times 4 = 8$.
Write 8 under the 9.

Step 3. Subtract: $9 - 8 = 1$.
Write 1 under the 8.

Step 4. Compare: 1 is smaller than 4.
The division is correct.

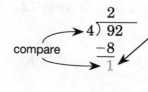

compare

To be correct, the difference (1) must be smaller than the divisor (4).

Step 5. Bring down the 2, and place it next to the 1.

Now repeat the 5 steps.

Step 1. Divide 4 into 12.
Write 3 over the 2.

Step 2. Multiply: $3 \times 4 = 12$.
Write 12 under the 12.

Step 3. Subtract: $12 - 12 = 0$.
Write 0 under the 12.

Step 4. Compare: 0 is smaller than 4.

Step 5. There is no other digit to bring down.

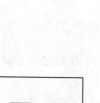

compare

0 shows no remainder. (You do not need to write this 0.)

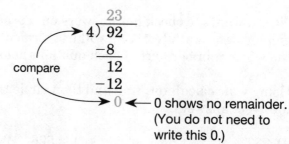

Calculator Solution of Example 1

Press Keys: C 9 2 ÷ 4 =

Answer: 23.

▼ **MATH TIP**

You can use your calculator to check the answer of a division problem.

Example 2:

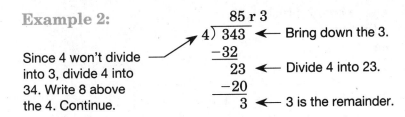

Since 4 won't divide into 3, divide 4 into 34. Write 8 above the 4. Continue.

$$
\begin{array}{r}
85 \text{ r } 3 \\
4\overline{)343} \quad \leftarrow \text{ Bring down the 3.} \\
-32 \\
\hline
23 \quad \leftarrow \text{ Divide 4 into 23.} \\
-20 \\
\hline
3 \quad \leftarrow \text{ 3 is the remainder.}
\end{array}
$$

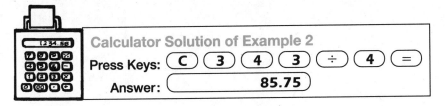

Calculator Solution of Example 2

Press Keys: (C) (3) (4) (3) (÷) (4) (=)

Answer: 85.75

▼ **MATH TIP**

You can use a calculator to check the *whole number part* of a quotient when there is a remainder.

▼ Practice

Divide. Complete the row of partially worked Skill Builders. Then solve the following problems.

Skill Builders

1.
$$
\begin{array}{r}
13 \\
4\overline{)55} \\
-4 \\
\hline
15 \\
-12
\end{array}
\qquad
\begin{array}{r}
1 \\
5\overline{)70} \\
-5 \\
\hline
20
\end{array}
\qquad
\begin{array}{r}
2 \\
6\overline{)164} \\
-12 \\
\hline
44
\end{array}
\qquad
\begin{array}{r}
2 \\
7\overline{)182} \\
-14 \\
\hline
42
\end{array}
\qquad
\begin{array}{r}
4 \\
9\overline{)389} \\
-36 \\
\hline
29
\end{array}
$$

Answers with No Remainders

2. $5\overline{)65¢}$ $7\overline{)98}$ $6\overline{)\$90}$ $5\overline{)75}$ $4\overline{)72}$

3. $8\overline{)184}$ $3\overline{)261}$ $6\overline{)564}$ $5\overline{)\$270}$ $8\overline{)296}$

Answers with Remainders

4. $2\overline{)33}$ $4\overline{)51}$ $6\overline{)73}$ $5\overline{)84}$ $8\overline{)99}$

5. $4\overline{)193}$ $6\overline{)284}$ $7\overline{)331}$ $9\overline{)565}$ $8\overline{)452}$

6. Tickets are selling in 4 locations for the upcoming rock concert. On the table below, divide to find how many tickets were sold per hour at each location during the hours indicated.

	Outlet Name	Number of Tickets Sold (a)	Hours Outlet Open (b)	Tickets Sold per Hour (a ÷ b)
a)	Fran's Bookstore	875	7	_____
b)	Music City	801	9	_____
c)	Owen's Market	575	5	_____
d)	Downtown Mall	984	4	_____

7. Charlie and his son work as garbage collectors on Wednesday, Thursday, and Friday. The table below shows the number of homes they service and the hours they work on each of these days.

Divide to find how many homes per hour Charlie and his son must serve if they are to keep on this work schedule.

	Day	Number of Homes (a)	Hours of Work (b)	Homes per Hour (a ÷ b)
a)	Wednesday	378	6	_____
b)	Thursday	456	8	_____
c)	Friday	531	9	_____

In problems 8 and 9, circle your answer choice.

8. Alice has 55 jelly beans to divide equally among her 4 children. She'll keep any left over for herself. How many jelly beans will Alice get?

a) 1
b) 2
c) 3

9. For the weekend sale at Royce's Hardware, Royce is making up some "3-Pound Assorted Nuts and Bolts" packages. How many of these packages can he make if he starts with 137 pounds of mixed nuts and bolts?

a) 45
b) 46
c) 47

▼ MATH TIP

A problem that asks you to find *per unit* (per hour, etc.) is a division problem.

Finding an Average

Paul bowls for his company's league team, The Friendly Market Timber Wolves. At the end of Saturday night's games, Paul wants to compute each of his team members' average score.

To compute an average score, Paul adds the scores of all the games played by that bowler. Then, he divides the sum of those scores by the number of games the bowler played.

Here's how Paul determined his own average score for Saturday night. Paul bowled 3 games that evening.

a) Add the 3 scores:

Game #1	148
Game #2	167
Game #3	+ 162
Total:	477

b) Divide by 3

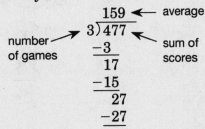

number of games → 3)477 ← sum of scores
159 ← average

▼ **MATH TIP**

An average is usually not equal to any of the numbers in the group you add.

However, the average is often close to the middle value of the group.

▼ **Practice**

Compute the average score for each bowler listed below.
As shown, bowlers did not all play the same number of games.

Name	Scores				Average Score
	Game #1	Game #2	Game #3	Game #4	
George	151	173	—	—	
Dottie	168	182	—	—	
Paul	148	167	162	—	159
Harry	160	182	192	—	
Helen	137	123	110	142	
Mario	185	163	179	189	

Dividing into Larger Numbers

Once you learn the 5 steps of division, you can divide any large number simply by repeating these steps.

Example: Divide: $4\overline{)1{,}579}$

1st division: divide 4 into 15.

Step 1. Divide: $15 \div 4 = 3$

Step 2. Multiply: $3 \times 4 = 12$

Step 3. Subtract: $15 - 12 = 3$

Step 4. Compare.

Step 5. Bring down the 7.

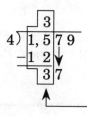

Compare
3 is smaller than the divisor 4.

2nd division: divide 4 into 37.

Step 1. Divide: $37 \div 4 = 9$

Step 2. Multiply: $9 \times 4 = 36$

Step 3. Subtract: $37 - 36 = 1$

Step 4. Compare.

Step 5. Bring down the 9.

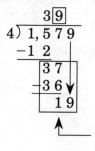

Compare
1 is smaller than the divisor 4.

3rd division: divide 4 into 19.

Step 1. Divide: $19 \div 4 = 4$

Step 2. Multiply: $4 \times 4 = 16$

Step 3. Subtract: $19 - 16 = 3$

Step 4. Compare.

Step 5. There is no other digit to bring down.

Answer: 394 r 3

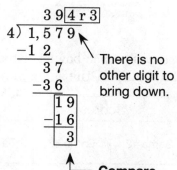

There is no other digit to bring down.

Compare
3 is the remainder and is smaller than the divisor 4.

▼ **MATH TIP**

Think of a long division problem as being made up of several short divisions.

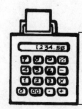

Calculator Solution of Example

Press Keys: C 1 5 7 9 ÷ 4 =

Answer: 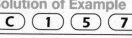 394.75

▼ Practice

Divide. Complete each row of partially worked Skill Builders. Then solve the following problems.

Answers with No Remainders

Skill Builders

Example

1.
$$\begin{array}{r} 124 \\ 7{\overline{)868}} \\ -7 \\ \hline 16 \\ -14 \\ \hline 28 \\ -28 \\ \hline \end{array}$$
$$\begin{array}{r} 16 \\ 6{\overline{)978}} \\ -6 \\ \hline 37 \\ -36 \\ \hline 1 \end{array}$$
$$\begin{array}{r} 2 \\ 4{\overline{)956}} \\ -8 \\ \hline 1 \end{array}$$
$$\begin{array}{r} 25 \\ 5{\overline{)1,265}} \\ -10 \\ \hline 26 \\ -25 \\ \hline 1 \end{array}$$
$$\begin{array}{r} 4 \\ 8{\overline{)3,712}} \\ -32 \\ \hline 5 \end{array}$$

2.
$3{\overline{)468}}$
$5{\overline{)\$740}}$
$4{\overline{)972}}$
$7{\overline{)833}}$
$9{\overline{)\$999}}$

3.
$6{\overline{)3,798}}$
$3{\overline{)2,631}}$
$7{\overline{)\$2,485}}$
$2{\overline{)1,374}}$
$8{\overline{)2,312}}$

Answers with Remainders

Skill Builders

Example

4.
$$\begin{array}{r} 147 \text{ r } 1 \\ 3{\overline{)442}} \\ -3 \\ \hline 14 \\ -12 \\ \hline 22 \\ -21 \\ \hline 1 \end{array}$$
$$\begin{array}{r} 14 \\ 5{\overline{)743}} \\ -5 \\ \hline 24 \\ -20 \\ \hline 4 \end{array}$$
$$\begin{array}{r} 1 \\ 6{\overline{)813}} \\ -6 \\ \hline 2 \end{array}$$
$$\begin{array}{r} 28 \\ 7{\overline{)2,011}} \\ -14 \\ \hline 61 \\ -56 \\ \hline 5 \end{array}$$
$$\begin{array}{r} 3 \\ 4{\overline{)1,543}} \\ -12 \\ \hline 3 \end{array}$$

5.
$5{\overline{)873}}$
$6{\overline{)749}}$
$4{\overline{)685}}$
$8{\overline{)3,537}}$
$7{\overline{)4,112}}$

Using Zero as a Place Holder

Use 0 as a place holder in the answer of a division problem each time you

- divide into 0
- divide into a number that is smaller than the divisor

Example 1: Divide $7\overline{)280}$

1st Division

```
     4
7) 280      Divide 7 into 28.
  -28
   00 ← Subtract. Bring down 0.
```

2nd Division

```
    40
7) 280
  -28
   00 ← Divide 7 into 00.
   00    00 (or 0) ÷ 7 = 0
         Write 0 in the answer.
```

Example 2: Divide $6\overline{)3,612}$

1st Division

```
     6
6) 3,612    Divide 6 into 36.
  -3 6
    01 ← Subtract. Bring down 1.
```

2nd Division

```
    602
6) 3,612  /   6 won't divide into 1;
  -3 6        write 0 in the answer.
    012 ← Bring down the 2, and
   -12    divide 6 into 12.
     0
         └ 0 shows no remainder.
```

Examples:

```
        500              3,000
5) 2,500          12) 36,000
  -2 5               -36
   000               0 000
  - 00              -  000
```

Divide.

1. $3\overline{)270}$ **3.** $7\overline{)490}$

2. $6\overline{)4,200}$ **4.** $5\overline{)\$75,000}$

Examples:

```
        502              3,005
7) 3,514          6) 18,030
  -3 5               -18
   014               0 030
  - 14              -  30
```

Divide.

5. $8\overline{)2,432}$ **7.** $6\overline{)5,442}$

6. $5\overline{)\$4,515}$ **8.** $7\overline{)14,063}$

Making Business Decisions

Imagine that you run a fast-food sandwich restaurant. You keep your prices low in order to be competitive. So, to make a profit, you must sell a lot of sandwiches and not have too many employees.

You know that to earn a profit, your restaurant must sell 500 sandwiches each week for each person you have working for you. When the average number of sandwiches sold per employee drops below 500, you do not make any money. You can't earn enough to pay for the cost of supplies, employee wages, and other expenses.

To see how to run your restaurant most profitably, you kept track of your weekly sales during a several-week trial period. You had a different number of employees work each week. Your results are shown on the table below.

	Number of Sandwiches Sold (a)	Number of Employees (b)	Number of Sandwiches Sold per Employee (a ÷ b)
1.	2,655	5	_____
2.	3,534	6	_____
3.	3,647	7	_____
4.	3,976	8	_____
5.	4,329	9	_____

▼ Practice

A. Divide the Number of Sandwiches Sold (a) by the Number of Employees (b). Write the quotient in the Number of Sandwiches Sold per Employee column.

B. If you plan to make a profit, what is the largest number of employees that you can have working in your restaurant?

Dividing Dollars and Cents

To divide dollars and cents, place the decimal point in the answer directly above its place in the dividend.

Example 1: 4)$3.76

Step 1. Put a decimal point directly above its place in the dividend and divide the numbers.

```
     .94
4) $3.76
   -3 6
     16
    -16
      0
```

Step 2. Place the dollar sign in the answer.

```
    $0.94
4) $3.76
      ↑
      └── Decimal points
          are lined up.
```

Example 2: Divide $0.72 by 8.

Step 1. Place the decimal point directly above its place in the dividend. Because 8 will not go into 7, put a zero after the decimal point.

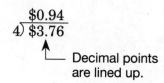

```
          8 goes into 7
          zero times.
     .0
8) $0.72
```

Step 2. Divide, and place dollar sign in the answer.

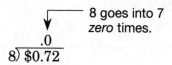

```
          8 goes into 72
          nine times.
    $0.09
8) $0.72
```

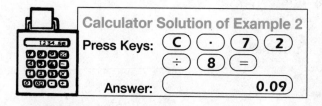

Calculator Solution of Example 2
Press Keys: (C) (·) (7) (2)
(÷) (8) (=)
Answer: 0.09

Divide.

1. 6)$2.58   **4.** 7)$9.24

2. 4)$12.40   **5.** 8)$16.08

3. 5)$2.55   **6.** 9)$28.98

_____

7. 7)$0.49   **10.** 6)$0.36

8. 4)$0.24   **11.** 9)$0.81

9. 8)$0.64   **12.** 5)$0.45

Computing the Lowest Unit Price

When Carrie shops, she is careful to check the **unit price** of each item she buys.

Carrie is more interested in saving money than she is in buying a particular brand name.

• To compute unit price, Carrie divides the total price by the number of units she buys.

Example: Which is Carrie's best buy on tomatoes?

    a) 5 pounds for $6.45
    b) 8-pound bag for $9.92
    c) 10-pound bag for $1.26 per pound

Carrie divides to compute price per pound:

Choice a	**Choice b**	**Choice c**
$1.29	$1.24	Given as
5)$6.45	8)$9.92	$1.26 per
−5	−8	pound.
1 4	1 9	
−1 0	−1 6	
45	32	
−45	−32	

Carrie decides that choice b, tomatoes at $1.24 per pound, is the best buy.

▼ **Practice**

Compute the unit price in each group below.
Circle each best buy. (Note: lb. = pound; oz. = ounce)

1. a) Price per pound: _____
    5 lb. $5.65

    b) Price per pound: _____
    6 lb. $6.54

    c) Price per pound: _____
    8 lb. $9.52

2. a) Price per ounce: _____
    4 oz.   OLIVES 4 OZ. $1.68

    b) Price per ounce: _____
    6 oz.   OLIVES 6 OZ. $2.34

    c) Price per ounce: _____
    8 oz.   OLIVES 8 OZ. $2.96

Dividing and Estimating

Many times when you divide, you'll need only an **estimate** of the answer. Most often, you'll estimate

- to find an approximate answer

- to choose from among answer choices on a test

- to check a calculator answer

To estimate a quotient, follow these steps:

- Divide to find the first digit of the estimate.

- Write 0s for any remaining digits.

Example 1: 7)591‾

Step 1. Divide to find the first digit.

$$\begin{array}{r} 8\,X \\ 7\overline{)5\,9\,1} \end{array}$$ Does 7 go into 5? <u>no</u>
Does 7 go into 59? <u>yes, 8 times</u>

Write 8 over the 9.
Write X over the 1.
(When estimating, ignore any remainder.)

Step 2. Write 0 in place of the X.
8X ⟶ 80

Estimate: 80 (exact answer is 84 r 3)

Example 2: 8)$171.04‾

Step 1. Divide to find the first digit.

$$\begin{array}{r} 2\,X.X\,X \\ 8\overline{)\$1\,7\,1.0\,4} \end{array}$$ Does 8 go into 1? <u>no</u>
Does 8 go into 17? <u>yes, 2 times</u>

Write 2 over the 7.
Write Xs over the remaining digits.
Correctly place the dollar sign and decimal point.

Step 2. Write 0s in place of the Xs.
$2X.XX ⟶ $20.00

Estimate: $20.00 (exact answer is $21.38)

In problems 1 and 2, write the first quotient digit in each box. Then change Xs to 0s to write each estimate.

Estimate   **Estimate**

1. $\square$X → _____ $\square$XX → _____
   6) 4 9 3   4) 5 3 7

2. $\square$XX → _____ $\square$X.XX → _____
   7) 1,5 0 9   4) $1 3 0.7 5

In problems 3 and 4, write an estimate for each quotient.

Estimate   **Estimate**

3. 4) 5 0 9   _____   6) $1 3 .9 8   _____

4. 8) 4,2 5 0   _____   3) $2 5 1.8 0   _____

5. Part of your job at Bryan's Market is to compute the unit price of certain foods.

   Use estimating to check the unit prices written below. Circle the three that are incorrect.

Food Item	Price & Size	Unit Price
Orange Juice Concentrate	8-ounce size for $0.96	$0.12 per ounce
Olives	8-ounce size for $2.56	$0.49 per ounce
Coffee	3-pound size for $7.29	$2.43 per pound
Chicken	5-pound pack for $5.45	$2.09 per pound
Salmon	7-pound fish for $29.33	$4.19 per pound
Cheese	2-pound size for $6.14	$3.34 per pound

▼ **MATH TIP**

People make math mistakes! And, because they do, they need a way to quickly check answers. Estimating is the best tool.

By estimating, you can catch mistakes in both pencil-and-paper answers and in calculator answers.

As problem 5 shows, estimating is most useful in catching mistakes that are "way off," rather than catching mistakes that are close.

Estimating with Larger Divisors

Possibly nowhere in math will you appreciate your ability to estimate more than when you're dividing 2-digit or larger divisors!

- The first step in estimating or in finding an exact answer is to decide where to place the first digit in the quotient.

Deciding Where to Start

Example 1: Divide

$$\overset{\text{X}}{28\overline{)252}}$$

Does 28 go into 2?   no
Does 28 go into 25?   no
Does 28 go into 252?   yes

Write an X over the second 2.

Conclusion: The exact answer has 1 digit and possibly a remainder.

Example 2: Divide

$$\overset{\text{XX}}{37\overline{)1{,}591}}$$

Does 37 go into 1?   no
Does 37 go into 15?   no
Does 37 go into 159?   yes

Write an X over the 9.
Write another X over the 1.

Conclusion: The exact answer has 2 digits and possibly a remainder.

> ### ▼ MATH TIP
>
> The first step in estimating in a division problem is to decide how many digits will be in the answer.

▼ Practice

Place Xs to show where the digits go in each quotient below. Then, without solving these problems, circle each exact answer from the choices given.

1. $19\overline{)494}$
   a) 6
   b) 26
   c) 106

2. $32\overline{)260}$
   a) 8 r 4
   b) 18 r 4
   c) 118 r 4

3. $45\overline{)928}$
   a) 2 r 28
   b) 20 r 28
   c) 200 r 28

4. $23\overline{)3{,}335}$
   a) 5
   b) 45
   c) 145

5. $17\overline{)19{,}735}$
   a) 16 r 15
   b) 116 r 15
   c) 1,160 r 15

6. $235\overline{)4{,}465}$
   a) 19
   b) 190
   c) 1,190

Estimating a Quotient

To estimate a quotient, follow these steps:

- Round the divisor.

- Divide to find the first digit.

- Write 0s for any remaining digits.

Example 3: Divide: $213\overline{)7{,}426}$

Step 1. Round the divisor to the nearest 100.

$$213 \longrightarrow 200 \quad 200\overline{)7{,}426}$$

Step 2. Divide to find the first digit of the estimate.

How many times does 200 go into 742?

Think:	Then Write:
$1 \times 200 = 200$	$3X$
$2 \times 200 = 400$	$200\overline{)7{,}4\,2\,6}$
↙ $3 \times 200 = 600$	
$4 \times 200 = 800$	

Step 3. Write a 0 in place of the X.
$$3X \longrightarrow 30$$

Estimate: 30 (exact answer is 34 r 184)

▼ Practice

Estimate each quotient below. The first problem in each row is done as an example.

7. $28\overline{)6\,3\,9}$ $\longrightarrow$ $\overset{2X \rightarrow 20}{30\overline{)6\,3\,9}}$
$$\begin{array}{r} -6\,0 \\ \hline 3 \end{array}$$
How many
30s in 63?

$19\overline{)8\,3\,7}$

$31\overline{)\$6\,4\,6}$

8. $13\overline{)4{,}8\,0\,4}$ $\longrightarrow$ $\overset{4XX \rightarrow 400}{10\overline{)4{,}8\,0\,4}}$
$$\begin{array}{r} -4\ 0 \\ \hline 8 \end{array}$$
How many
10s in 48?

$12\overline{)6{,}2\,2\,5}$

$31\overline{)\$6{,}4\,5\,2}$

9. $113\overline{)8{,}7\,5\,0}$ $\longrightarrow$ $\overset{8X \rightarrow 80}{100\overline{)8{,}7\,5\,0}}$
$$\begin{array}{r} -8\ 0\,0 \\ \hline 7\,5 \end{array}$$
How many
100s in 875?

$192\overline{)4{,}3\,7\,8}$

$278\overline{)13{,}0\,5\,7}$

Estimating in the Workplace

Phil Branson works as a bookkeeper for Carl's School Supplies. Part of Phil's job is to keep track of current amounts of items that Carl's sells.

When supplies drop below the "3-month point," Phil orders more supplies from the manufacturers. In this way, Carl's always has enough supplies in its warehouse to meet customers' needs.

Phil doesn't need to know exact numbers of supplies on a day-to-day basis. So, he uses estimating. If his estimate tells him that Carl's has only 3 months' worth (or less) of supplies remaining, Phil calls the manufacturer.

Here's an example. Phil knows there are about 210 cases of paper glue in the warehouse. He also knows that Carl's sells an average of 19 cases of paper glue each month. Phil divides to estimate the number of months these supplies of glue will last.

Exact   **Estimate**

$$19\overline{)210} \rightarrow 20\overline{)210}^{1X} \rightarrow 10 \text{ months}$$

With 10 months' supply remaining, Phil does not place an order at this time.

▼ Practice

1. Complete the following table for Phil. Check "Yes" in the **To Order** column only when **Estimated Supply (in months)** is 3 months or less. Estimate to find your answer.

Inventory					
Date: January 3					
Item	Currently In Warehouse (a)	Average Monthly Shipment (b)	Estimated Supply (in months) (a ÷ b)	To Order Yes	No
Dictionaries	1,895	850	____	____	____
World Almanacs	2,950	590	____	____	____
Colored Markers	580 boxes	187	____	____	____
Paper Glue	210 cases	19	10	____	✓
Typing Paper	3,694 boxes	288	____	____	____
Typewriters	57	11	____	____	____
Desk Chairs	19	8	____	____	____

When an order arrives from a manufacturer, Phil checks the invoice. The invoice tells what is contained in the order, and it tells what total amount Carl's is being charged.

By dividing the **total cost** by the **number** of items **received**, Phil figures out how much each item costs. Because factory prices quite often change without notice, Phil is interested only in approximate costs. He estimates to determine each approximate cost.

For example, Phil received an order of 412 calculators at a total cost of $2,190.24. He divides to estimate the amount that Carl's is being charged per calculator.

Exact   **Estimate**

$$\text{5.XX} \longrightarrow \$5.00$$
$$412\overline{)\$2,1\,9\,0.2\,4} \longrightarrow 400\overline{)\$2,1\,9\,0.2\,4}$$

Carl's is paying about $5.00 per calculator.

2. Complete the table of estimates below for Phil.

Item	Total Cost (a)	Number Received (b)	Estimated Unit Cost (a ÷ b)
Calculators	$2,190.24	412	$5.00
Earth Globes	$1,604.65	67	_____
File Cabinets	$651.90	8	_____
Slide Projectors	$636.60	19	_____
Pencil Sharpeners	$410.85	83	_____
Staplers	$123.60	28	_____
Computer Printers	$4,662.80	11	_____

3. Last year Phil worked 40 hours per week for a total of 50 weeks. For this work, he earned a gross yearly salary of $15,346.

a) How many total hours did Phil work last year?_____

b) Estimate Phil's hourly pay rate for last year. _____

Dividing by a Two-Digit Number

The same 5 steps that are used to divide by a single digit are used to divide by a two-digit, or larger, number.

- As shown below, estimating can help you with the first step.

Example: Divide: $18\overline{)829}$

1st division: divide 18 into 82.

Step 1. Ask, "How many times does 18 go into 82?"

Estimate to find out:

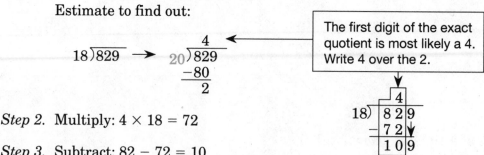

The first digit of the exact quotient is most likely a 4. Write 4 over the 2.

Step 2. Multiply: $4 \times 18 = 72$

Step 3. Subtract: $82 - 72 = 10$

Step 4. Compare: 10 is smaller than 18

Step 5. Bring down the 9, and place it next to the 10.

2nd division: divide 18 into 109.

Step 1. Ask, "How many times does 18 go into 109?"

Because 109 is larger than 82, you know that 18 goes into 109 four or more times. Try 5 and 6.

$$
\begin{array}{r}
4\,6\ \text{r}\ 1 \\
18\overline{)829} \\
-72 \\
\hline
109 \\
-108 \\
\hline
1 \leftarrow \text{remainder}
\end{array}
$$

Try 5	**Try 6**
18	18
$\times\,5$	$\times\,6$
90	108 ✔ 6 is correct.

Step 2. Multiply: $6 \times 18 = 108$

Step 3. Subtract: $109 - 108 = 1$

Step 4. Compare: 1 is smaller than 18

Step 5. There is no other digit to bring down.

Answer: 46 r 1

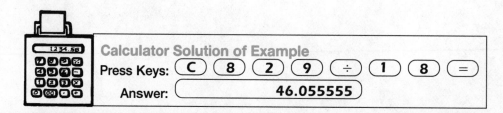

Calculator Solution of Example

Press Keys: C 8 2 9 ÷ 1 8 =

Answer: 46.055555

Adjusting the Quotient

Sometimes, even when using an estimate as a guide, you write an incorrect digit in the quotient. When this happens, increase or decrease the digit as needed.

Here are three examples.

Example 1
quotient digit is too small

$$\begin{array}{r} 5 \\ \cancel{4} \\ 26\overline{)131} \\ -104 \\ \hline 27 \end{array}$$

27 is larger than 26, so add 1 to the 4 and multiply with the 5.

Example 2
quotient digit is too large

$$\begin{array}{r} 1 \\ \cancel{2} \\ 44\overline{)826} \\ -88 \end{array}$$

88 is larger than 82, so subtract 1 from the 2 and multiply with the 1.

Example 3
quotient digit is correct

$$\begin{array}{r} 3 \\ 32\overline{)982} \\ -96 \\ \hline 2 \end{array}$$

The digit 3 in the quotient is correct. The difference 2 is less than 32.

▼ Practice

Check to see if each quotient digit is correct. Cross out each incorrect digit, and write the correct digit above it.

1.

$$\begin{array}{r} 2 \\ 27\overline{)82} \end{array}$$

$$\begin{array}{r} 4 \\ 19\overline{)94} \end{array}$$

$$\begin{array}{r} 5 \\ 35\overline{)211} \end{array}$$

$$\begin{array}{r} 9 \\ 24\overline{)197} \end{array}$$

2.

$$\begin{array}{r} 7 \\ 41\overline{)321} \end{array}$$

$$\begin{array}{r} 8 \\ 72\overline{)690} \end{array}$$

$$\begin{array}{r} \$0.07 \\ 46\overline{)\$3.68} \end{array}$$

$$\begin{array}{r} \$0.09 \\ 16\overline{)\$1.44} \end{array}$$

Check   Check   Check   Check

3.

$$\begin{array}{r} 17 \\ 22\overline{)352} \\ -22 \\ \hline 132 \end{array}$$

$$\begin{array}{r} 23 \\ 17\overline{)408} \\ -34 \\ \hline 68 \end{array}$$

$$\begin{array}{r} 17 \\ 38\overline{)646} \\ -38 \\ \hline 266 \end{array}$$

$$\begin{array}{r} \$0.25 \\ 13\overline{)\$3.12} \\ -26 \\ \hline 52 \end{array}$$

Divide. Complete the row of partially worked Skill Builders. Then solve the following problems.

Skill Builders

4.

$$\begin{array}{r} 2 \\ 29\overline{)63} \\ -58 \end{array}$$

$$\begin{array}{r} 5 \\ 25\overline{)129} \end{array}$$

$$\begin{array}{r} 1 \\ 26\overline{)442} \\ -26 \\ \hline 18 \end{array}$$

$$\begin{array}{r} 3 \\ 31\overline{)1,054} \\ -93 \\ \hline 12 \end{array}$$

6.
$$\begin{array}{r} \\ 34\overline{)\$230.86} \\ -204 \\ \hline 26 \end{array}$$

Answers with No Remainders

5. $13\overline{)52}$ $16\overline{)\$96}$ $25\overline{)125}$ $22\overline{)154}$ $32\overline{)\$16.00}$

6. $16\overline{)432}$ $38\overline{)798}$ $27\overline{)486}$ $25\overline{)\$3,125}$ $14\overline{)\$68.46}$

Answers with Remainders

7. $15\overline{)79}$ $24\overline{)95}$ $37\overline{)283}$ $26\overline{)372}$ $47\overline{)967}$

8. $19\overline{)1,685}$ $35\overline{)4,150}$ $63\overline{)7,926}$ $24\overline{)3,824}$ $53\overline{)23,769}$

9. Divide the Sales Amount by the Number of Days of Sale to find the Average Sales per Day.

Sales Amount	Number of Days of Sale	Average Sales per Day
$41,106.00	12	_____
$73,500.00	28	_____
$77,715.00	36	_____

Keeping a Mileage Record

Suppose you work for McCarthy Distributors. Part of your job is to keep track of the gas mileage of each of the company's vehicles. This information is used to help decide when each vehicle is in need of a tune-up.

The gas mileage of each vehicle is checked on the first day of each month. To compute it, you do the following:

- compute the **monthly miles**—the number of miles the vehicle was driven that month

- divide monthly miles by the **monthly gas use**—the number of gallons of gas used by the vehicle that month

The mileage of each vehicle is recorded on the partially completed **Monthly Mileage Record** shown below.

Here's how you compute the **Gas Mileage** of vehicle C48 for the **Monthly Mileage Record** below.

a) Compute monthly miles:

Subtract: June 1 reading: 32,574
  − May 1 reading: − 30,486
  2,088 ← monthly miles

b) Divide monthly miles by monthly gas use. You can use your calculator.

$$\begin{array}{r} 29 \\ 72\overline{)2,088} \\ -1\,44 \\ \hline 648 \\ -648 \end{array}$$ ← gas mileage

---

▼ Practice

Complete the Monthly Mileage Record below. You can use your calculator.

Monthly Mileage Record

Vehicle Number	Mileage Reading May 1 (a)	June 1 (b)	Monthly Miles (b − a) = c	Monthly Gas Use (in gal.) (d)	Gas Mileage (miles per gal.) (c ÷ d)
1. C48	30,486	32,574	2,088	72	29
2. C53	18,641	20,305	_____	64	_____
3. C79	27,671	30,368	_____	87	_____
4. T77	41,308	42,043	_____	49	_____
5. T93	52,796	53,134	_____	26	_____

Shortcuts in Division
Dividing Numbers That End in Zero

Here is a shortcut for dividing numbers that end in one or more zeros:

- Take an equal number of 0s off both the divisor and the dividend.

- Divide the numbers that remain.

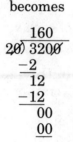

$$20 \overline{)3200}$$

Take 1 zero off both numbers.

Example: During the last 20 days, Evan has driven his car 3,200 miles. On the average, how many miles did Evan drive each day?

becomes

$$\begin{array}{r} 160 \\ 2\!\!\!/0 \overline{)3200\!\!\!/} \\ -2 \\ \overline{12} \\ -12 \\ \overline{00} \\ 00 \end{array}$$

To solve this problem, divide 3,200 by 20. Using the shortcut, you simply divide 320 by 2.

Answer: 160

▼ Practice

Use the shortcut and divide.

Skill Builders

1. $30 \overline{)60} \longrightarrow 3\!\!\!/0 \overline{)6\!\!\!/0}$ $70 \overline{)280} \longrightarrow 7\!\!\!/0 \overline{)28\!\!\!/0}$ $200 \overline{)11000} \longrightarrow 2\!\!\!/0\!\!\!/0 \overline{)110\!\!\!/0\!\!\!/0}$

2. $20 \overline{)\$80}$ $40 \overline{)160}$ $30 \overline{)180}$ $60 \overline{)420}$ $80 \overline{)3,200}$

3. $200 \overline{)800}$ $300 \overline{)900}$ $400 \overline{)1600}$ $600 \overline{)\$1800}$ $500 \overline{)9000}$

4. $400 \overline{)8,000}$ $200 \overline{)18,000}$ $300 \overline{)\$15,000}$ $200 \overline{)20,000}$ $700 \overline{)49,000}$

Dividing by 10, 100, or 1,000

The shortcut gives us 3 easy rules to use when dividing certain numbers by 10, 100, or 1,000.

- To divide a number that ends in one or more 0s by 10, take one 0 off that number.

$$500 \div 10 = 50$$

take off one 0

- To divide a number that ends in two or more 0s by 100, take two 0s off that number.

$$2,400 \div 100 = 24$$

take off two 0s

- To divide a number that ends in three or more 0s by 1,000, take three 0s off that number.

$$13,000 \div 1,000 = 13$$

take off three 0s

Divide.

5. $80 \div 10 =$ 　　　　　　$\$350 \div 10 =$ 　　　　　　$700 \div 10 =$

6. $400 \div 100 =$ 　　　　　$\$5,000 \div 100 =$ 　　　　$23,400 \div 100 =$

7. $6,000 \div 1,000 =$ 　　　$\$14,000 \div 1,000 =$ 　　$72,000 \div 1,000 =$

For problems 8–10, circle your answer choice.

8. During the first half of this year, the 100 members of the Hazelton Dieters Club lost a total of 2,800 pounds. What was the average amount of weight lost by each dieter?

a) 28 pounds
b) 280 pounds
c) 2,800 pounds

9. The final 500 donations to the local United Way fund-raising drive totaled $16,000. On the average, how much was contributed by each donator?

a) $3.20
b) $32.00
c) $320.00

10. The distance from the earth to the moon is about 240,000 miles. Flying at a speed of 4,000 miles per hour, how many hours would it take a spacecraft to travel from the earth to the moon?

a) 6
b) 60
c) 600

Putting It All Together

Working with a Budget

To help keep track of expenses, many families prepare a household budget. A budget contains both **fixed expenses** and **variable expenses**.

- Fixed expenses are costs such as car payments that don't change each month.

- Variable expenses are costs such as food that may change each month.

With fixed expenses, you can predict exactly how much monthly expenses will be. With variable expenses, you can only guess. However, a fairly accurate guess can be made if a several-month average is computed.

The Winslow family has listed their fixed and variable expenses on the tables in the following exercises.

▼ Practice

In this exercise, you will review what you have learned about dividing whole numbers and money.

To find fixed costs

1. a) For each yearly fixed cost, divide by 12 to determine the monthly fixed cost.
    b) For each 6-month fixed cost, divide by 6 to determine the monthly fixed cost.
    c) Add to find the Total Monthly Fixed Costs.

Fixed Costs		
Item	**Yearly Fixed Cost**	**Monthly Fixed Cost**
Rent	$4,620.00	_____
Car Payment	$2,224.80	_____
Health Insurance	$950.40	_____
	6-Month Fixed Cost	
Car Insurance	$238.80	_____
Property Insurance	$105.00	_____
	TOTAL	_____

To find variable costs

2. a) Add to find each 3-month total. Then divide by 3 to find the Average Monthly Variable Cost.
   b) Add the Average Monthly Variable Cost column to find the Total.

You can use your calculator.

	Variable Costs				
Item	May (a)	June (b)	July (c)	3-Month Total (a + b + c) = d	Average Monthly Variable Cost (d ÷ 3)
Electric Power	$24.80	$21.70	$22.05	_____	_____
Gas Heat & Water Heater	$49.60	$38.00	$28.80	_____	_____
Car Gas & Oil	$58.00	$64.50	$55.25	_____	_____
Clothes	$72.40	$70.30	$88.90	_____	_____
Food	$194.80	$182.50	$185.95	_____	_____
Entertainment	$54.00	$62.00	$46.00	_____	_____
				TOTAL	_____

To find estimated monthly costs

3. Add the Total Monthly Fixed Costs (answer 1c) and the Total Average Monthly Variable Costs (answer 2b).

   Total Monthly Costs = _____
   (fixed + variable)

4. The Winslow family has a monthly take-home income of $1,482.80. After subtracting their total monthly costs (answer 3), how much money do they have left over for other expenses and savings? _____

5. The Winslows are thinking about buying a second car. The purchase price of the car is about $11,150. They plan to put $1,000 down and pay off the balance in equal monthly payments.
   a) What will be the balance owed after the Winslows subtract the down payment? _____
   b) Not counting interest, **estimate** what the Winslows' monthly payment would be if they paid off the balance in 4 years (48 months)? _____

Measurement of Time

Do you manage your time well?

Nancy looked at the clock on her office wall. Two forty-five, she thought. Let's see now. I have to pick up Rita at day care at 4:00. Malcolm gets out of after-school care at 4:30 and has to be at soccer practice forty-five minutes later. It will take me about a half hour to do the grocery shopping for dinner. Do I have time to finish this last memo, or should I do the shopping now and work tonight? Or maybe I should finish the memo now and take Rita shopping with me while Malcolm is at practice. But will I have enough time to get from the store to the soccer field by the end of practice? Nancy groaned out loud. "I need a graduate degree in time management to figure out my schedule," she announced to her co-workers.

Think About It

- Why is Nancy frustrated?

- Do you sometimes get frustrated with your daily schedule? What kinds of things help? What makes the situation worse?

How Does Time Play a Part in *Your* Life?

Think about your daily routine. There are probably some things you do every day, some things you do once or twice a week, and other things that you only do occasionally. Answer the questions that follow to see how different your life would be without <u>time</u>.

On the spaces below, write down the things you do <u>every</u> day and the time of day that you do them.

Activity	Time
_____	_____
_____	_____
_____	_____
_____	_____
_____	_____

Have you ever been late for an appointment? What made you late? What happened as a result?

_____

_____

Imagine that you want to be somewhere at a certain time. How do you decide what time you should leave?

_____

_____

Do you wear a watch? About how many times do you look at it each day?

_____

_____

Skills You Will Learn

Number Skills
- reading a clock
- adding and subtracting time

Life and Workplace Skills
- reading a bus schedule
- computing weekly pay
- using a calendar
- understanding time zones

Thinking Skills
- planning ahead
- scheduling

Reading a Clock

Keeping track of the **hours and minutes** of each day may be the most common measurement most of us make.

The hands of the clock below display hours and minutes.

- Reading the shorter **hour hand,** each number represents 1 hour.

- Reading the longer **minute hand,** each number represents 5 minutes.

Writing Time

hour ——— minutes after the hour

5:12

a colon separates hours from minutes

Time: twelve minutes after five

- Always write two digits after the colon, even if both digits are 0.

3:00

three o'clock

4:09

nine minutes after four

▼ MATH TIP

- Except when the minute hand is on the 12, the hour hand is between two clock numbers.
- Since each number represents 5 minutes when you are reading the longer hand, count by 5s to determine the number of minutes before or after the hour.

$5 \times 5 = 25$, so the time is 8:25.

▼ Practice

Using numbers and a colon, write the time shown on each clock.

1.

_____

3.

_____

5.

_____

2.

_____

4.

_____

6.

_____

Finding Earlier and Later Times

Ernie's boss said, "Be here 45 minutes early tomorrow. We're having a meeting."

Ernie wondered, "I usually start work at 9:30 A.M. What time should I be here tomorrow?"

Being able to determine earlier and later times is an important skill. Your job may depend on it.

Remember:

* A.M. refers to hours between midnight and noon.

* P.M. refers to hours between noon and midnight.

Example 1: It's now 4:45 P.M. What time will it be in 35 minutes?

> **Think:** In 15 minutes it will be 5:00 P.M.
> In 20 more minutes it will be 5:20 P.M.

Answer: 5:20 P.M.

35 min. later

Example 2: How long is it until the noon lunch break if it is now 10:15 A.M.?

> **Think:** In 45 minutes it will be 11:00 A.M.
> In 1 hour more it will be 12:00 P.M.

Answer: 1 hour 45 minutes

noon

Example 3: It's now 8:45 A.M. What time will it be in 5 hours and 20 minutes?

> **Think:** In 5 hours it will be 1:45 P.M.
> In 20 more minutes it will be 2:05 P.M.

Answer: 2:45 P.M.

Example 4: Jules is supposed to come to work 50 minutes early tomorrow. His normal workday starts at 9:30 A.M. What time should he arrive tomorrow?

> **Think:** 30 minutes before 9:30 A.M. is 9:00 A.M.
> 20 minutes before 9:00 A.M. is 8:40 A.M.

Answer: 8:40 A.M.

50 min. earlier

▼ Practice

Find an earlier or later time than the time shown.

1.

Time Now

_____ 45 minutes later

2.

Time Now

_____ 50 minutes earlier

3.

Time Now

_____ 3 hr. 35 min. later

4.

Time Now

_____ 2 hr. 20 min. earlier

5. On the chart at right, Aida is keeping track of the hours she was at work during the three days shown.

Complete this chart for her. The Monday hours are done as an example.

Day	Hours Worked
Monday	8 hr. 30 min.
Tuesday	_____
Wednesday	_____

Monday: **Arrive**   **Leave**
                A.M.   P.M.

Aida thinks:

8:30 A.M. to noon: 3 hr. 30 min.
noon to 5:00 P.M.   5 hr.
Add to find total: 8 hr. 30 min.

Tuesday: **Arrive**   **Leave**
               A.M.   P.M.

Wednesday: **Arrive**   **Leave**
                 A.M.   P.M.

IN YOUR LIFE

Reading a Bus Schedule

Imagine that you ride the bus to and from work each day and when you want to go downtown to shop. To some extent, you must organize your time around the **bus schedule** shown below.

Bus Schedule #14 Downtown/Highland				
LEAVE Highland Station	20th & Lark	50th & James	80th & Lincoln	ARRIVE Downtown Station
7:05 A.M.	7:18	7:29	7:40	7:46
8:15	8:28	8:39	8:50	8:56
9:21	9:34	9:45	9:56	10:02
10:25	10:38	10:49	11:00	11:06
11:10	11:23	11:34	11:45	11:51

▼ Practice

1. You look at your watch, shown at right. How long do you have to wait until the next bus leaves the Highland Station?

2. About how many minutes does it take the bus to go from the stop at 50th & James to the Downtown Station?

3. On Thursday, at 9:15 A.M., you are waiting to catch the bus at the Highland Station. A person working at the station puts up the following sign:

   "Buses are running 20 minutes late today."

   At what time can you expect to catch the next bus?

4. If you catch the 9:34 bus at 20th & Lark, how many minutes will it take you to get to the Downtown Station?

169 ◀

Computing Weekly Pay

To make sure she is paid the correct amount, Glenda decided to compute her weekly **gross pay** (pay before taxes). Glenda earns $7.00 for each of her first 40 hours of work; she earns $10.50 for each overtime hour ($5.25 for each 30 minutes of overtime).

Glenda has listed the time she worked last week at right.

Total Hours and Minutes Worked

Monday	7 hr.	45 min.
Tuesday	8 hr.	30 min.
Wednesday	8 hr.	45 min.
Thursday	7 hr.	45 min.
Friday	9 hr.	45 min.
	39 hr.	**210 min.**

Finding Total Hours Worked

To find the total hours she worked, Glenda adds the hours and minutes columns:
> **Total:** 39 hr. 210 min.

To write 210 min. as hours and minutes, Glenda divides by 60 (60 min. = 1 hr.). The remainder gives the number of minutes left over.
> 210 min. = 3 hr. 30 min.

Rewriting 210 min.

$$\begin{array}{r} 3 \text{ hr. } 30 \text{ min.} \\ 60\overline{)210} \\ -180 \\ \hline 30 \end{array}$$

Now, to write total hours worked, Glenda adds 39 hr. and 3 hr. 30 min.
> **Total:** 42 hr. 30 min. (42 hr. 30 min. can be thought of as 40 hr. and 2 hr. 30 min.)

Answer: Glenda worked 40 regular hours and 2 hours 30 minutes of overtime.

Total Hours Worked

$$\begin{array}{r} 39 \text{ hr.} \\ + \ \ 3 \text{ hr. } 30 \text{ min.} \\ \hline 42 \text{ hr. } 30 \text{ min.} \end{array}$$

Computing Gross Pay

Glenda computed her total gross pay as follows:

Total Regular Pay

For 40 Hours

$$\begin{array}{r} \$7.00 \\ \times \ \ \ 40 \\ \hline \$280.00 \end{array}$$

Total Overtime Pay

For 2 Hours

$$\begin{array}{r} \$10.50 \\ \times \ \ \ \ 2 \\ \hline \$21.00 \end{array}$$

For 2 Hours and 30 Minutes

$$\begin{array}{r} \$21.00 \\ + \ \$5.25 \ \longleftarrow \text{ for 30 min. of overtime} \\ \hline \$26.25 \end{array}$$

Total Gross Pay

$$\begin{array}{r} \$280.00 \ \longleftarrow \text{ regular pay} \\ + \ \ \ 26.25 \ \longleftarrow \text{ overtime pay} \\ \hline \$306.25 \end{array}$$

Answer: Glenda earned a total of $306.25 last week.

Listed below are Glenda's scheduled work hours for next week. Assume that Glenda is paid for her lunch break, and that she works each of the days shown.

1. Determine the number of hours Glenda is scheduled to work each day. Write each daily total in the **Daily Hours** column.

2. Add the **Daily Hours** column to find the **Total Time for Week**. Simplify this time to hours and minutes—where the number of minutes is less than 60. (See how 210 minutes was changed to 3 hr. 30 min. on page 170.)

3. Determine:

   Total Regular Hours: _____ hours

   Total Overtime Hours: _____ hours _____ minutes

4. Determine:

   Total Regular Pay: $_____

   Total Overtime Pay: $_____

   Total Gross Pay: $_____
   (regular + overtime)

Scheduled Work Hours			
Day	Arrive	Depart	Daily Hours
Monday	8:00 A.M.	3:45 P.M.	7 hr. 45 min.
Tuesday	8:00 A.M.	5:30 P.M.	_____
Wednesday	8:00 A.M.	4:15 P.M.	_____
Thursday	8:30 A.M.	4:00 P.M.	_____
Friday	9:30 A.M.	5:30 P.M.	_____
Saturday	7:30 A.M.	11:00 A.M.	_____

Total Time for Week: _____ = _____ hr. _____ min.

Using a Calendar

Maria Hernandez fills out a **calendar** at the beginning of each month to help her remember important days such as work days, birthdays, meetings, and so on.

On the calendar below, Maria has filled out information she wants to remember during May.

MAY

SUN.	MON.	TUES.	WED.	THURS.	FRI.	SAT.
	1	2	Call Emma 3	4	5	4 hr. overtime 6
7	8	9	office meeting 9:00AM 10	11	12	13
MOTHER'S DAY 14	15	16	Sister's Birthday 17	18	19	3 hr. overtime 20
21	VICTORIA DAY CANADA 22	23	24	25	Write to Jason 26	27
28	MEMORIAL DAY 29	30	31			

Regular scheduled work day

▼ Practice

1. How many regular scheduled workdays is Maria planning to work during May?

   _____

2. Maria earns $6.50 per hour during regular work hours. She works 10 hours each regular scheduled workday. How much will Maria earn during regular workdays during May?

   _____

3. If Maria earns $9.75 for each overtime hour, how much overtime pay will she earn during May?

   _____

4. Fill out the June calendar below for Maria.

- Place a large X on each of Maria's regular workdays: each Tuesday, Wednesday, Thursday, and Friday.

- Write "6 hours overtime" on the third Saturday in June.

- Write "Office Meeting, 9:00 A.M." on the second Tuesday in June.

- Write "Rose's Birthday" on June 18.

5. How many days will Maria be going to work during the month of June?   _____

6. Compute each of the following:

a) total number of regular work hours Maria will work during June   _____

b) total amount of regular pay Maria will earn during June (at $6.50 per hour)   _____

c) total amount of overtime pay Maria will earn during June (at $9.75 per hour)   _____

d) total pay (regular + overtime) Maria will earn during June   _____

JUNE						
SUN.	MON.	TUES.	WED.	THURS.	FRI.	SAT.
				1	2	3
4	5	6	7	8	9	10
11	12	13	14	15	16	17
18	19	20	21	22	23	24
25	26	27	28	29	30	

Understanding Time Zones

The United States lies in 6 main time zones.
Looking at the map below, you see that:

- Hawaii is two hours earlier, and Alaska is one hour earlier than the states in the Pacific standard time zone.

- States in the Pacific standard time zone are three hours earlier than states in the eastern standard time zone.

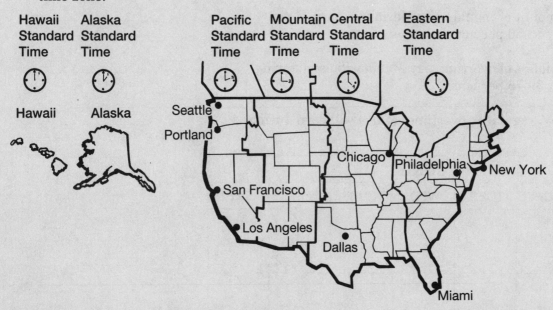

▼ Practice

Using the time zone map, answer these questions:

1. When it is 5:00 P.M. in Los Angeles, what time is it in Hawaii?

2. When the sun is coming up at 6:30 A.M. in Portland, Oregon, what time is it in Chicago?

3. If Na places a call at 1:45 P.M. Dallas, Texas, time, what time will her brother Tuan pick up the phone in Miami, Florida?

4. Jeri flew from Seattle, Washington, to Philadelphia. She left Seattle at 9:30 A.M., and the flight took 5 hours. What time was it in Philadelphia when she arrived?

Directions: The problems below represent many of the skills that you have learned in *Math Skills That Work, Book One*. Take your time and answer each question carefully. When you are finished, check your answers on page 198.

Unit One: Becoming Familiar with Numbers (Pages 1–25)

Problems 1–3 refer to the following information from a computer screen. As a data-entry clerk, you are responsible for entering information into the computer and retrieving information when necessary.

Date	Invoice Number	Balance Due	Company
8/20	7986	$4,280.12	Coastal Copier
9/23	8907	$1,876.90	Nan's Secretarial
9/27	9008	$114.08	Towson Supplies
10/10	9020	$4,190.00	Electric Alley

1. What is the invoice number of the oldest invoice listed?

2. If invoices are filed by invoice number, in which of the file drawers below would you find the invoice for Towson Supplies?

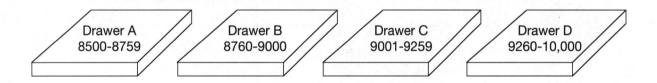

Drawer A
8500-8759

Drawer B
8760-9000

Drawer C
9001-9259

Drawer D
9260-10,000

3. List the amounts due in order from the **largest balance** due to the **smallest balance** due.

_____   _____   _____   _____

Turn to next page.

Problems 4–8 refer to the following menu and tax table. As an employee in a doughnut shop, you fill customer orders and make sure you receive the correct amount of money for the products sold.

Ricardo's Doughnut Shop		
Plain Doughnut – – – – – – – – –		$.37
Jelly-Filled Doughnut – – – – – – –		.46
Cholesterol-Free Doughnut – – –		.50
Jumbo Doughnut – – – – – – – –		.62
Coffee – – – – – – – – –	Small	.59
	Medium	.75
	Large	.92

Tax Table	
Amount of Purchase	Tax
$0.00 - $.99	$0.00
1.00 - 1.60	0.07
1.61 - 3.00	0.14
3.01 - 3.49	0.21

4. A customer buys 2 plain doughnuts, a jumbo doughnut, and a large cup of coffee. Fill out the sales slip below.

RICARDO'S			
Item	Quantity	Unit Price	Total Cost
		Subtotal	
		Tax	
		Total	

5. The customer pays for the purchases in problem 4 with a $5 bill. Circle the coins and bills that you should give him as change.

6. Another customer orders a cholesterol-free doughnut, a small coffee, and a large coffee. Fill out the sales slip below.

RICARDO'S			
Item	Quantity	Unit Price	Total Cost
		Subtotal	
		Tax	
		Total	

7. The customer pays for the purchases in problem 6 with three $1 bills. Circle the coins that he should receive in change.

8. A customer wants to buy one of each kind of doughnut listed on the menu. Before she does, she asks you to *estimate how much the bill will come to. Estimate the cost before tax.*

_____

Turn to next page.

Problems 9–11 refer to the following checking account register. Imagine that these transactions are yours and that you want to keep a very accurate record of your money.

Account #ED98721

RECORD ALL CHARGES OR CREDITS THAT AFFECT YOUR ACCOUNT

NUMBER	DATE	DESCRIPTION OF TRANSACTION	PAYMENT/ DEBIT	✔ T	FEE (IF ANY) (−)	DEPOSIT/ CREDIT (+)	BALANCE $ 557 90	
211	9/18	Big W. Grocery	$ 93 15		$	$		
	9/18	machine withdrawal	20 00					
212	9/21	Alfredo Davis	400 00					
	9/22	paycheck deposit				419 57		
213	9/25	Southwest Electric	31 17					

9. Compute the amount of money (balance) in your checking account after each transaction. Write each balance in the Balance column.

10. On September 27, you write a check (#214) to Corner Currency Exchange for $50.15.

11. On September 27, you also deposit a rebate check for $9.80. Record these transactions in problems 10 and 11 and find the balance in your account.

Unit Four: Multiplication (Pages 90–127)

Problems 12–15 refer to the following page from the inventory report for a convenience store. As a clerk, Dan is responsible for counting products on the shelves and in the stockroom once a week.

Product	# of Cartons on Shelves	# of Cartons in Stockroom	# of Units per Carton	Total # of Units
Andy's Chocolates	3	10	100	_____
Crunchers Candy	4	8	100	_____
Evertop Batteries	1	5	12	_____
Flavorite Bubble Gum	10	25	240	_____
Flavorite Gum	8	20	240	_____
Pocket Pens	1	2	50	_____
Three-Layer Bars	1	5	100	_____

12. For each product, determine the total number of units, and write each amount in the Total column.

13. If Dan sold all of the gum that is currently on the shelves (not including bubble gum), how many packages of gum would there be in the store? _____

14. Each of the following sells for $1.25: Andy's chocolates, Crunchers candy, and three-layer bars. How much money will the store take in from the sale of all of these products in stock (on the shelves and in the stockroom)? _____

15. The store has decided not to carry pens any longer. If the store sells an average of 10 pens each day, in how many days will the pen stock run out? _____

Turn to next page.

Problems 16–20 refer to the following information from a grocery store shelf. You are shopping for the ingredients to make chili, and as a wise consumer, you want to get the best value for your dollar.

Moline Kidney Beans 8 oz. $1.12	**Moline Kidney Beans** 12 oz. $1.56	**Moline Kidney Beans** 16 oz. $2.24

Suprema Tomato Sauce 10 oz. 70¢ $0.70	**Suprema Tomato Sauce** 12 oz. 72¢ $0.72	**Suprema Tomato Sauce** 16 oz. $1.12

Unit Five: Division (Pages 128–163)

16. Calculate the price per ounce of all three sizes of kidney beans. Write down the size that is the best value. __________

17. Calculate the price per ounce of all three sizes of tomato sauce. Write down the size that is the best value. __________

18. Your recipe calls for 48 ounces of kidney beans. You buy the size that is the best value. How much do you spend?__________

19. You also buy 4 cans of tomato sauce. You choose the size with the lowest unit price. How much do you save by not buying 3 sixteen-ounce cans?

20. In addition to the cost of the tomato sauce and kidney beans, you pay $1.19 for onions and $5.90 for ground beef. Your recipe serves 8 people. Estimate the total cost per serving.

____

Turn to next page.

Problems 21–25 refer to the following family financial information. Like most families, the Reeds have a certain income and certain "fixed" costs. In addition, they have costs that vary from month to month.

INCOME
Kerry Reed's Take-Home Pay: $17,040 per year
Chris Reed's Take-Home Pay: $10,380 per year

FIXED COSTS
Rent: $455/month
Car Payment: $140.40/month
Insurance: $750/year

VARIABLE COSTS	January	April	August	Estimated Average
Electricity	$25.80	$19.93	$20.05	
Gas Heat	52.90	41.88	38.15	
Gas and Oil for Car	34.82	32.91	51.76	
Food	354.00	361.54	378.12	
Clothing	41.00	57.00	67.00	

21. Estimate the monthly average of each variable cost listed on the chart. Write the average in the column provided. To estimate, round each amount to the nearest dollar.

22. What is the combined *monthly* take-home pay for Kerry and Chris?

23. How much is their monthly insurance payment? _____

24. Estimate the total amount of money they paid out in January. To find this estimate, round each amount to the nearest ten dollars before adding.

_____

25. After they made their January payments, approximately how much money did they have left over from that month's income to put into savings? _____

Turn to next page.

Problems 26 –28 refer to the following train schedule.

TRAIN	Departure Time			
	South Station (LV)	Kendall Corner	North Street	Central Station (AR)
#121	7:30 A.M.	7:50 A.M.	8:15 A.M.	8:30 A.M.
#160	7:50 A.M.	8:10 A.M.	8:35 A.M.	8:50 A.M.
#182	8:00 A.M. Express	------------------		8:45 A.M.
#190	8:15 A.M.	8:35 A.M.	9:00 A.M.	9:15 A.M.

26. You take the train from South Station to Central Station. How much time do you save by taking the express (#182) rather than any other morning train? _____

27. Today you have an errand to do in Kendall Corner before going to work. You take the #121 from South Station. What train should you take from Kendall in order to arrive at Central Station before 9:00? _____

28. You woke up yesterday morning and saw it was the time shown on the clock below. How much time do you have to get to the #190 train at South Station? _____

Answer Key

Unit One: Becoming Familiar with Numbers

The First Four Place Values

Page 3

1. 9
2. 34
3. 143
4. 305
5. 1,227
6. 1 ten, 7 ones
7. 4 tens, 9 ones
8. 1 hundred, 5 tens, 0 ones
9. 7 hundreds, 4 tens, 8 ones
10. 1 thousand, 5 hundreds, 3 tens, 8 ones
11. 4 thousands, 0 hundreds, 9 tens, 5 ones
12. 8 thousands, 6 hundreds, 4 tens, 0 ones

Writing Whole Numbers

Pages 4–5

A. 1. A830-245   3. B005-481
    2. A970-168   4. C624-978
B. 1. seventeen   6. ninety
    2. fourteen   7. three hundred
    3. twelve   8. four hundred
    4. forty   9. seven thousand
    5. fifty   10. nine thousand
C. 1. $38   3. $215   5. $1,872
    2. $46   4. $389
D. 1. twenty-one
    2. forty-eight
    3. one hundred ninety-two
    4. three hundred five
    5. six thousand
    6. five thousand, ninety
    7. seven thousand, eight hundred forty
    8. thirty-five
    9. seventy-two
   10. two hundred fifty-six
   11. eight hundred two
   12. nine thousand
   13. four thousand, forty
   14. nine thousand, three hundred sixty

Writing Dollars and Cents

Page 7

1. $7.09   9. 5¢, $.05 or $0.05
2. $23.06   10. 8¢, $.08 or $0.08
3. $41.08   11. 2¢, $.02 or $0.02
4. $72.25   12. 7¢, $.07 or $0.07
5. $112.90   13. 46¢, $.46
6. $204.61   14. 83¢, $.83
7. $550.30   15. 79¢, $.79
8. $900.02   16. 21¢, $.21

17. six dollars and nine cents
18. eight dollars and ninety-two cents
19. fourteen dollars and five cents
20. seventy-four dollars and fifty-three cents
21. one hundred fifty-six dollars and seventy-eight cents
22. three hundred fifty-seven dollars and forty cents
23. one thousand, thirty-two dollars and fifty cents
24. one thousand, five hundred six dollars and ninety cents

In Your Life

Pages 8–9

In Your Life
Pages 8–9 (continued)

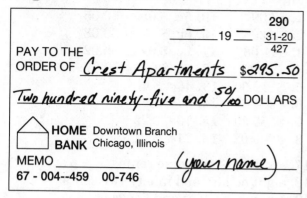

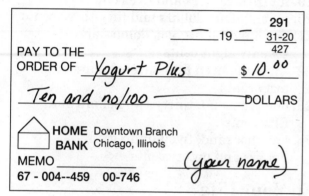

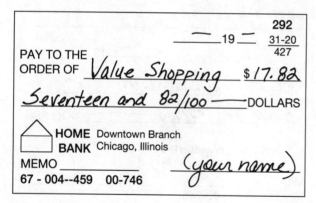

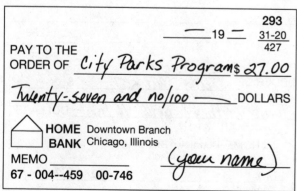

Comparing Numbers
Pages 10–11

1. B, A, C
2. C, B, A
3. 1384, 1386, 1387, 1388, 1390, 1391, 1392, 1393

Comparing Numbers
Pages 10–11 (continued)

4. $0.39 per lb.
5. $1.76
6. $8.92
7. $13.79
8. Adamly: $96.00
   James: $225.00
   Lerronde: $28.50
   Phillips: $45.75
   Smythe: $143.65
9. largest: James; smallest: Lerronde
10. Phillips
11. James

On the Job
Pages 12–13

1. B
2. A
3. C
4. B
5. C
6. A
7. 1711
8. 1719, 1721
9. 1765, 1768
10. 1802, 1834
11. none
12. C149, C153
13. 1st: $7,500.00, C150
    2nd: $4,462.75, C147
    3rd: $3,217.48, C152
    4th: $3,205.25, C148
    5th: $1,850.00, C151
    6th: $1,685.50, C154

In Your Life
Page 15

1. d
2. a
3. e
4. f
5. b
6. c
7. 3, N
8. 6, N
9. 12, S
10. 4, N
11. 34, S
12. 47, S

13.

| 420 | 494 | | 524 | 588 | | 618 | 698 |

California Avenue

| 443 | 499 | | 541 | 597 | | 645 | 695 |

← Downtown

Writing Dates as Numbers
Pages 16–17

1. 6/19/78 — 0 6 1 9 7 8
2. 12/13/85 — 1 2 1 3 8 5
3. 4/3/91 — 0 4 0 3 9 1
4. & 5. Answers will vary.
6. July 9, 1960
7. March 17, 1982
8. August 20, 1991
9. May 31, 1979
10. December 5, 1993
11. A. a-3, b-4, c-2, d-1, e-5
    B. a-4, b-2, c-5, d-1, e-3
12. a) 3/18/83
    b) 12/05/83
    c) 4/15/84
    d) 7/12/84

Understanding Larger Numbers
Pages 18–19

1. 45, 390
2. 93, 57
3. 250, 0
4. 734, 825
5. 6, 540, 300
6. 9, 450, 950
7. 45, 750, 0
8. 75, 125, 600
9. 245, 800, 0
10. 650, 985, 450

A. 1-d, 2-c, 3-f, 4-e, 5-a, 6-g, 7-h, 8-b

B.
1. 9,500
2. 5,140
3. 42,600
4. 58,960
5. 135,700
6. 394,570
7. 5,800,000
8. 9,450,300
9. 26,045,000
10. 280,500,000

C. 11. ninety-nine million, nine hundred ninety-nine thousand, nine hundred ninety-nine
12. two hundred forty-eight million, seven hundred fifty thousand

Rounding Whole Numbers
Page 21

Answers for 1–4 may vary. Representative answers are given.

1. 10
2. 10,000
3. 10
4. 1,000,000
5. 70, 300, 4,000
6. 40, 900, 7,000
7. $50, $400, $2,000
8. 150, 2,000, 12,000
9. 80
10. $1,500
11. $11,000
12. 240,000
13. 93,000,000

Rounding Dollars and Cents
Page 22

1. $1.00
2. $8.00
3. $3.00
4. $3.00
5. $40.00
6. $180.00
7. $70.00
8. $190.00

Focus on Calculators
Page 25

Answers will vary. Representative answers are given.

1. solar (if solar cells present), battery (if no solar cells)
2. ON/OFF
3. "0."
4. a) 8   b) 99,999,999
5. C
6. "0."
7. a) 27.
   b) 540.
   c) 4895.
   d) 6.98
   e) 0.75
8. ON/OFF

Focus on Calculators
Page 25 (continued)

9. a) yes   b) yes   c) yes

Unit Two: Addition

Adding Single Digits
Pages 28–30

1. 3 + 4 = 7 or   3
                 + 4
                 ——
                  7
2. 4 + 2 = 6 or   4
                 + 2
                 ——
                  6
3. 1 + 3 = 4 or   1
                 + 3
                 ——
                  4
4. 6, 9, 7¢, 9, 9, 8¢
5. 4, $8, 8, 6, 7¢, 9
6. 7, 7, 9, $5
7. 15, 13, $10, 11, 11, 12
8. 15¢, 14, 12, 14, 16, 10
9. 14, 17, 15, $15
10. 18, 16, $13, 13
11. 7
12. 7
13. 11
14. 10
15. A. 1-h, 2-f, 3-g, 4-d, 5-b, 6-a, 7-e, 8-c
    B. 1-e, 2-c, 3-g, 4-b, 5-d, 6-h, 7-f, 8-a
16. 18, 19, 17, 15
17. 16, 17, 15, 13
18. 17, 16, 14, 15
19. 4,6 3,7 2,8 1,9
20. 5,5 8,2 7,3 6,4

Adding Three or More Digits
Page 31

1. 14, 12, 17, 20, 17, 18
2. 24, 19¢, 15, 21, $15, 19
3. 17¢, 24, 12, 27, 20, $19
4. 19, 17, 16¢, 13, 15, 17
5. $20
6. $21

Focus on Calculators
Page 33

A. 1. C 4 7 + 3 9 =
   2. C 4 · 1 7 + 2 · 1 5 =
   3. C 2 6 4 5 + 1 3 5 0 =
   4. C 5 9 + 4 2 + 3 6 =

B. 1. 58, 179, 627, $2,396, $10.37
   2. 92, 324, 769, $3,533, $22.92
   3. March: $1,018.20
      April: $942.43
      May: $895.44

Adding Larger Numbers
Pages 34–35

1. 18, 88, $88, 289, 999, 848
2. $89, 98, 589, 888, $3,897, 8,985
3. 4,788 lb.

Adding Larger Numbers
Pages 34–35 (continued)

A. 1. 30	**5.** 78	**B. 1.** 598
2. 39	**6.** 186	**2.** 789
3. 179	**7.** 1,967	**3.** 868
4. 68	**8.** 668	**4.** 698

Adding Dollars and Cents
Pages 36–37

1. $6.79, $2.88, $8.79
2. $17.78
3. $19.44
4. $6.66
5. $3.98
6. $1.85
7. $3.69
8. 59¢
9. $7.97
10. 99¢, $0.99
11. 83¢, $0.83
12. 97¢, $0.97
13. 85¢, $0.85
36¢, $0.36
76¢, $0.76
14. 16¢, $0.16
47¢, $0.47
67¢, $0.67
15. $21.26 $6.06 $11.85
16. $26.16 $16.36 $36.56

Choosing Information You Need
Pages 38–39

1. c
2. c
3. c
4. b
5. b
6. A-b, B-c, $4.86
7. A-b, B-c, $569
8. A-a, B-c, 337

Reading a Table
Pages 40–41

1. 480
2. 48 g
3. 52 g
4. ham
5. ham
6. ham
7. a
8. b
9. 12 ounces
10. 580 calories
11. 17 g

In Your Life
Pages 42–43

A. 1. 1,095 calories
2. hamburger, cheeseburger
3. 1st: fish 2nd: chicken
3rd: hamburger 4th: cheeseburger
B. 1. 425, 240, 647
2. a) dinner **b)** lunch
3. 1,312
4. a) 359 **b)** 453

Adding and Carrying
Pages 44–46

1. 43, 95¢, 100, 86, $141
2. 35, 56¢, 102, $106, 93¢
3. 47, 53¢, 92, 93, 222

Adding and Carrying
Pages 44–46 (continued)

4. 416; 719; 746; 519; 829
5. $555; 469; 933; 828; 977
6. 668; $879; 508; $1,216; 1,418
7. 7,197; 6,795; 9,276; 13,197; 21,996
8. 6,439; 7,260; $5,795; 13,582; 14,437
9. 4,994; 6,997; 9,589; 12,069; $23,298
10. 270; 743; 3,932; 769; 5,510
11. 630; $761; 3,557; 6,641; 8,432
12. $656; 586; 2,782; 8,735; 13,338
13. Burrell: 2,517 lb. Dart: 3,752 lb.
Jenkins: 4,147 lb. Smith: 4,970 lb.
Garcia: 5,095 lb.

Estimating Answers
Pages 47–48

1. 70¢
2. 80 pens
3. $12.00
4. 900 miles
5. $10,000
6. b
7. d
8. 1,000, 965
9. 10,000, 10,293
10. $900, $900

Estimating and Shopping
Page 49

Grocery Costs
1. $2
2. $3
3. $1
4. $3
5. $5
6. $4
7. $7
8. $12
Total: $37

Clothing Costs
1. $8
2. $4
3. $15
4. $12
5. $8
6. $40
7. $4
8. $43
Total: $134

Hardware Costs
1. $2
2. $6
3. $8
4. $13
5. $10
6. $5
7. $3
8. $1
Total: $48

Auto Parts Costs
1. $10
2. $4
3. $7
4. $40
5. $2
6. $2
7. $70
8. $3
Total: $138

Carrying with Dollars and Cent
Pages 50–51

1. $4.86, $6.36, $4.94
2. $10.47
3. $4.72
4. $4.77

5. $8.18, $8.55, $8.29   **12.** $3.41
6. $4.19   **13.** $7.00, $6.87
7. $16.39   **14.** $7.00, $7.35
8. $7.49   **15.** $500, $507.28
9. $8.34   **16.** $2.00, $1.88
10. $1.97   **17.** $10.00, $10.02
11. $3.44   **18.** $9,000, $9,274.74

Adding Coins
Page 53

1. 30¢   **5.** $1.26   **9.** Answers may vary:
2. $1.25   **6.** $2.40   3 quarters, 1 dime,
3. 90¢   **7.** $1.32   1 nickel
4. $1.50   **8.** $2.38   **10.** Answers may vary:
                                    6 quarters, 1 dime,
                                    1 nickel

On the Job
Pages 54–55

A. 1. $3.22   **2.** $3.36   **3.** yes

B.

JERRY'S RESTAURANT				
Table No.	No. persons	Bill No.	Server No.	
cheeseburger			1	89
large soda				74
fries, small				59
pie			1	09
Subtotal			4	31
Tax				22
Total			4	53

Jason's new bill

Skill Review
Pages 56–57

Answers 1–4

Catalog Order Form

	Catalog Number	Description	Price
1.	3682	fitted sheet	$17.84
2.	3686	flat sheet	14.77
3.	3690	pillow	7.99
4.	3786	pillow case	4.85
5.	3790	thermal blanket	16.49
6.	3795	bedspread	68.00
		Subtotal:	$129.94
		Amount of Tax:	6.50
		Total Cost:	$136.44

Skill Review
Pages 56–57 (continued)

Answer 5

Catalog Order Form

	Catalog Number	Description	Price
1.	3690	pillow	$7.99
2.	3786	pillow case	4.85
3.	3790	thermal blanket	16.49
4.			
5.			
6.			
		Subtotal:	$29.33
		Amount of Tax:	1.47
		Total Cost:	$30.80

Unit Three: Subtraction

Subtracting Small Numbers
Pages 60–62

1. $8 - 2 = 6$ or
$$\begin{array}{r} 8 \\ -2 \\ \hline 6 \end{array}$$

2. $6 - 3 = 3$ or
$$\begin{array}{r} 6 \\ -3 \\ \hline 3 \end{array}$$

3. $4 - 2 = 2$ or
$$\begin{array}{r} 4 \\ -2 \\ \hline 2 \end{array}$$

4. 5, 4¢
5. 5, 3
6. $2, 2
7. 9, 8¢
8. 7¢, 4

9. 6, $7
10. 2, 5, 6, 4, $2, 4
11. 4, 4¢, 5, 2, 4, $1
12. 0, 3, $3, 3, 3, 5
13. 7, 3¢, 8, 9, 7, 4
14. $3, 5, 9, 9¢, 9, 6
15. 9, $7, 9, 8, 8, 6¢
16. A. 1-h, 2-e, 3-f, 4-c,
           5-d, 6-g, 7-a, 8-b
     B. 1-f, 2-d, 3-e, 4-a,
           5-g, 6-b, 7-h, 8-c
17. 6, $2, 3
18. 3, 0, 3¢

Focus on Calculators
Page 64–65

A. 1. C 1 7 4 − 8 9 =
    2. C 2 5 · 0 0 − 1 9 · 7 8 =
    3. C 1 · 8 7 − · 9 7 =
    4. C 2 3 8 6 − 1 5 7 9 =
B. 1. 23, 18, $1.27, $2.90, 1,453
    2. 37, 31, 234
    3. $2.10, $6.60
    4. Profit: $133.85
C. 1. Double Keying, C 3 8 + 1 9 =
    2. Transposed Digits,
           C 6 2 − 4 3 =
    3. Wrong Key, C 9 4 + 5 8 =
    4. Transposed Digits,
           C · 8 7 + · 2 9 =
    5. Wrong Key, C 7 5 + 4 6 =

Subtracting Larger Numbers
Pages 66–67

1. 11¢, 24, 13, 51¢, 16, 23
2. 123, 118, $120, 51, 130, 231
3. $333, 410, 1,225, 541, $2,132, 3,330
4. 1,101 lb.
5. A. 1. 3,007   B. 1. 3,150
    2. 3,840   2. 2,494
    3. 2,452   3. 1,813
    4. 3,259   4. 4,121
    5. 3,266   5. 933

Subtracting Dollars and Cents
Page 68

1. $2.62, $6.62, $4.20
2. $11.75
3. $15.50
4. $3.44
5. $1.52
6. $2.10
7. $4.25
8. $3.20
9. $1.11
10. 22¢, $0.22
11. 33¢, $0.33
12. 41¢, $0.41

Subtracting Coins
Page 69

1. 40¢   2. $1.10   3. $1.10   4. $1.25

Understanding a Paycheck Stub
Page 71

A. 1. $5.20   5. $78.99
   2. $7.80   6. a) $78.99 + $16.18 + $37.43
   3. $486.20   + $14.85 + $12.66
   4. $326.09   b) $486.20 − $326.09
B. 1. $2.60   3. $62.81   5. $160.11, yes
   2. 89   4. $160.11

In Your Life
Page 72
Interpreting a Charge-Card Statement

1. $293.22   2. $132.12   3. $161.10   4. yes

Page 73
Keeping Track of Charge-Card Spending

1.
Date	Description	Charges	Payments + credits	Balance
4/1	Beginning Balance			$376.81
4/3	New Hat (Hat Shoppe)	$12.99		389.80
4/6	Gasoline (Towne Gas)	11.75		401.55
4/9	payment		$100.00	301.55
4/11	Groceries (Best Food Store)	44.85		346.40
4/13	Return of Blouse		23.20	323.20
4/24	Gasoline (Robert's)	13.00		336.20
4/25	payment		120.00	216.20
4/27	medical supplies	27.50		243.70

Page 73
Keeping Track of Charge-Card Spending (continued)

2. $110.09   3. $243.20   4. $133.11

Subtracting by Borrowing
Pages 74–76

1. 28; 15; 19; 35; 216
2. 28¢; 34; 28; 35¢; 28
3. 18; $18; 218; 303; 205
4. 341; 664; 242; 552; 173
5. $553; 182; 367; $662; 282
6. 91; 191; 536; 181; $253
7. 1,615; 721; 3,510; 3,530; 4,811
8. 4,647; 1,430; $6,951; 4,121; 1,811
9. $3,344; 442; 4,943; $3,922; $4,800
10. 559; 278; 287; 379; 1,755
11. 439; $535; 78; 188; 278
12. 2,087; 3,088; 529; $1,875; 2,446

13.
Week of June 8		Name: Jan Kincaid	
Date	Odometer Begins	Odometer Ends	Daily Mileage
6/8	9,278	9,659	381
6/9	9,659	9,957	298
6/10	9,957	10,348	391
6/11	10,348	10,712	364
6/12	10,712	11,097	385
6/13	11,097	11,498	401
6/14	11,498	11,850	352
		Weekly Total:	2,572

Subtracting and Estimating
Page 77

1. c   4. a) 50, correct   c) 2,000, correct
2. b   b) 400, incorrect d) 4,000, incorrect
3. b

Subtracting from Zero
Pages 78–79

1. 114, 100   275, 300   1,091, 1,000
2. 189, 200   315, 300   296, 300
3. 2,617, 3,000   3,038, 3,000   2,665, 3,000
4. 222, 200   1,215, 1,200   3,032, 3,000
5. 114, 100   191, 200   474, 500
6. 1,161, 1,200   2,518, 3,000   2,715, 3,000

Subtracting from Zero
Pages 78–79 (continued)

7. a) $71, $100 **d)** $1,766, $2,000
   b) $113, $100 **e)** $1,106, $1,000
   c) $121, $100 **f)** $1,893, $2,000

Borrowing with Dollars and Cents
Pages 80–81

A. 1. $1.17, $2.02
   2. $2.16
   3. $1.75
   4. $1.16
   5. $1.61, $3.50
   6. $0.35
   7. $5.75
   8. $4.82
   9. $0.70 or 70¢

   10. $2.53
   11. $1.11
   12. $4.24

B. 1. $1.00, $1.11
   2. $8.00, $8.08
   3. $2.00, $2.13
   4. $16.00, $15.61
   5. $2.00, $1.75
   6. $3.00, $2.98

On the Job
Pages 82–83

Answers may vary on each part *b*.

1. a) $6.11
   b) 1 five-dollar bill, 1 one-dollar bill, 1 dime, 1 penny
2. a) $3.74
   b) 3 one-dollar bills, 2 quarters, 2 dimes, 4 pennies
3. a) $5.93
   b) 1 five-dollar bill, 3 quarters, 1 dime, 1 nickel, 3 pennies
4. a) $6.83
   b) 1 five-dollar bill, 1 one-dollar bill, 3 quarters, 1 nickel, 3 pennies
5. Correct change should be $6.59. Change given is too *little* by $0.18.
6. Correct change should be $7.87. Change given is too *much* by $0.15.

On the Job
Pages 84–85

Answers may vary.

1. Correct change: 2 pennies, 1 nickel, 1 quarter, 3 one-dollar bills, and 1 five-dollar bill
2. Correct change: 2 pennies, 1 nickel, 1 dime and 1 quarter

On the Job
Pages 84–85 (continued)

3. Correct change: 1 penny, 1 dime, 2 quarters
4. Correct change: 1 penny, 2 quarters, 2 one-dollar bills
5. Correct change: 1 penny, 1 dime, 2 quarters, and 1 five-dollar bill
6. Correct change: 3 quarters, 3 one-dollar bills, and 1 ten-dollar bill
7. Correct change: 1 nickel, 1 dime, 1 five-dollar bill, 1 ten-dollar bill, and 1 twenty-dollar bill

In Your Life
Page 87

Answers 1, 2, & 3

CHECK REGISTER
RECORD ALL CHARGES OR CREDITS THAT AFFECT YOUR ACCOUNT

NUMBER	DATE	DESCRIPTION OF TRANSACTION	PAYMENT /DEBIT	✓	FEE (IF ANY)	DEPOSIT /CREDIT	BALANCE
							675.00
310	5/1	Elm Street Apts. #335.00					335.00
							340.00
311	5/4	Big Three Market	27.68				27.68
							312.32
	5/7	cash withdrawal at bank	40.00				40.00
							272.32
312	5/10	Northern Power Co.	108.39				108.39
							163.93
	5/16	payroll deposit				525.00	525.00
							688.93
313	5/17	Brennar's Furniture	82.50				82.50
							606.43
314	5/21	Al's Auto	65.00				65.00
							541.43
315	5/22	Corner Market	21.50				21.50
							519.93
316		Void					—
							519.93
317	5/27	New Hope Bank	467.00				467.00
							52.93
	5/28	Cash Withdrawal	25.00				25.00
							27.93
	5/29	payroll deposit				525.00	525.00
							552.93
	5/30	service charge	8.50				8.50
							544.43

REMEMBER TO RECORD AUTOMATIC PAYMENTS/DEPOSITS ON DATE AUTHORIZED

4. a) Write a note in the check register, dated May 31 and correct the balance at that point.
   b) $626.93

Skill Review
Pages 88–89

Answers 1 & 2 & 3d

PASSBOOK OF: (your name)				
DATE	WITHDRAWALS	INTEREST	DEPOSITS	BALANCE
6/1				$341.82
6/2			$98.62	440.44
6/23	$65.75			374.69
6/30		$2.09		376.78
7/3			62.00	438.78
7/9	28.00			410.78
7/14			145.00	555.78
7/28	50.00			505.78
7/29			9.30	515.08

3. a) $16.05   **b)** $9.30

c)

CASH	CURRENCY	9	00
	COIN		30
LIST CHECK SINGLY			
TOTAL		9	30

Unit Four: Multiplication

Multiplying Single Digits
Page 92

1. $3 \times 4 = 12$ **2.** $2 \times 8 = 16$

Basic Multiplication Facts
Page 94

1. 2, 4, 6, 8, 10, 12, 14, 16, 18
2. 3, 6, 9, 12, 15, 18, 21, 24, 27
3. 4, 8, 12, 16, 20, 24, 28, 32, 36
4. 5, 10, 15, 20, 25, 30, 35, 40, 45

5. 20	**8.** 45	**11.** 8	**14.** 32
6. 21	**9.** 36	**12.** 27	**15.** 24
7. 28	**10.** 18	**13.** 10	**16.** 35

Counting by 6s and 7s
Page 95

1. 36	**6.** 35	**11.** $3 \times 6 = 18$
2. 24	**7.** 42	**12.** $6 \times 7 = 42$
3. 21	**8.** 48	**13.** $0 \times 7 = 0$
4. 63	**9.** $4 \times 5 = 20$	**14.** $6 \times 5 = 30$
5. 49	**10.** $5 \times 7 = 35$	

Counting by 8s and 9s
Pages 96–97

1. 48	**6.** 36	**11.** $6 \times 8 = 48$
2. 64	**7.** 32	**12.** $9 \times 6 = 54$
3. 81	**8.** 27	**13.** $8 \times 4 = 32$
4. 63	**9.** $8 \times 5 = 40$	**14.** $9 \times 5 = 45$
5. 54	**10.** $9 \times 7 = 63$	**15.** $6 \times 7 = 42$

16.

1	2	3	4	5	6	7	8	9	10
2	4	6	8	10	12	14	16	18	20
3	6	9	12	15	18	21	24	27	30
4	8	12	16	20	24	28	32	36	40
5	10	15	20	25	30	35	40	45	50
6	12	18	24	30	36	42	48	54	60
7	14	21	28	35	42	49	56	63	70
8	16	24	32	40	48	56	64	72	80
9	18	27	36	45	54	63	72	81	90
10	20	30	40	50	60	70	80	90	100

17.

Monday	$36
Tuesday	48
Wednesday	30
Thursday	54
Friday	42
Saturday	36
Gross Pay:	$246

Multiplying by One Digit
Pages 98–99

1. 96, 24, 84, $90, 77, 69¢
2. 129, $305, 560, 108, 729, $128
3. 693, 644, $822, 639, 648, 690
4. 1,896; 3,248; 4,088; 2,884; $6,377; 2,080
5. b
6. a
7. b
8.

Rent	$930
Electricity	96
Gas	186
Car Payment	630
Insurance	159
Food	930
Telephone	66
Total 3-Month Expenses	$2,997

c) $3,960
d) $963 ($3,960 − $2,997)

Focus on Calculators
Page 101

A. 1. Ⓒ④⑦✕①⑨═
2. Ⓒ①•⑧⑨✕⑦═

Focus on Calculators
Page 101 (continued)

A. 3. ⓒ⑨✕⑧✕⑦⊜
  4. ⓒ·⑧⑨✕①②✕④⊜

B. 1. 72, 315, 4,095
  2. 216, 672, 37,638
  3. $61.92, $34.08, $660.00
  4. 1. Envelopes $ 720
       2. Stamps   2,250
       3. Pencils   130
       4. Pens   445
       5. Typing Paper   370
       6. Phone Calls   2,250
       Total Yearly Costs $6,165

Multiplying and Carrying
Pages 102–105

1. 56; 84; 235; 472; 681; 2,496
2. 84¢; 48; $81; 148; 301; 468
3. 608; $294; 576; 696; 387; $1,070
4. 627; 848; 1,535; 4,554; 3,240
5. 648; 824; 2,745; $4,864; 4,854
6. 429; 968; 1,750; 1,686; 5,200
7. 608; 489; $840; 968; 782
8. $1,448; 2,349; 3,426; $5,440; 988
9. 7,290; 6,048; 7,269; 32,200; 70,290
10. 13,680; $12,055; 10,569; 11,600; 19,640
11. 28,866; 27,300; 48,600; $37,680; 62,377
12. c   **13.** b   **14.** d   **15.** a
16. 1.   360   **17.** 1. 13,680
     2.   540   2. 23,400
     3.   588   3.   5,769
     4.   496   4. 18,880
     5.   486   5. 35,460
     6.   384
Total: 2,854 sq. yd.

Carrying to Two or More Columns
Page 106

1. 771; 1,304; 4,476; 8,832; 29,472
2. 438; $316; 980; 2,838; $4,224
3. 5,700; 4,602; 17,965; $30,058; 15,018

Being Sure an Answer Makes Sense
Page 107

1. $1,800, c   **3.** 32,000, d
2. 5,000, b   **4.** $210,000, a

Multiplying with Dollars and Cents
Page 108

1. $6.69,   **4.** $116.00   **8.** $2.45
    $12.52,   **5.** $116.97   **9.** $2.73
    $10.15   **6.** $1.83   **10.** $6.00
2. $33.75   **7.** $2.88   **11.** $7.92
3. $39.40

Estimating with Dollars and Cents
Page 109

1. $3.00, c   **4.** $50.00, b   **7.** $35.00, c
2. $8.00, a   **5.** $8.00, b   **8.** $192.00, a
3. $72.00, a   **6.** $9.00, b

In Your Life
Pages 110–111

1. 2 Cheeseburgers $2.38
    1 Heavenly Double   1.79
    3 Small Fries   2.64
    1 Dinner Salad   1.29
    3 Large Soft Drinks   2.37
    1 Large Coffee   .95
          Total: $11.42

2. 2 Heavenly Singles $2 × $1.00 = $2.00
    1 Chicken Sandwich   1 × $2.00 = $2.00
    3 Dinner Salads   3 × $1.00 = $3.00
    3 Small Fries   3 × $1.00 = $3.00
    3 Large Milks   3 × $1.00 = $3.00
              Total: $13.00

3. a)

Meal #1

Estimate	Exact
$3.00	$3.57
1.00	1.25
3.00	3.87
$7.00	$8.69

Meal #2

Estimate	Exact
$3.00	$2.97
3.00	2.64
3.00	2.55
$9.00	$8.16

b) The estimate for meal #2 is more than the exact price.

c) The estimate for each item in meal #1 is less than the actual price of each item. That is why the estimate for meal #1 is low. The opposite is true for the estimate for meal #2—where the estimate for each item is higher than the actual price.

Multiplying Numbers That End in Zero
Pages 112–113

1. 2,100; 3,000; 15,000; 350,000; 1,800,000
2. 1,000; 3,200; $4,500; 8,000; $12,000
3. 40,000; 1,400,000; $665,000; $120,000; $189,000
4. a) $2,400   f) $24,000
   b) $4,500   g) $15,000
   c) $2,700   **Total of Estimated**
   d) $20,000   **Receipts:** $248,600
   e) $180,000
5. #1 90   #2 270   #3 1,000   #4 600
   #5 9,800   #6 15,000   #7 10,000
   #8 26,000   #9 30,000

Multiplying by Two Digits
Pages 114–115

1. 2,747; 1,680; 2,250; 19,092; 27,907
2. $374; 1,032; 944; $2,482; 5,580
3. 7,056; 19,875; $29,212; 25,854; 30,973
4.

Truck #	Estimate	Incorrect
M417	24,000	X
M675	35,000	X
M298	16,000	
M318	30,000	X
M587	24,000	
M638	21,000	
M274	15,000	X

In Your Life
Page 117

1. A & B Foods: $13.73 *best buy
   Freddy's: $15.29
   Ervin's: $14.88
2. Save More: $11.76
   Home Foods: $11.62
   Shoppers Plus: $11.46 *best buy

3. $10.41 discount

On the Job
Pages 118–119

1. $ 115.50
2.   179.50
3.   114.00
4.   1,142.40
5.   898.80
6.   519.00
7.   400.35
8. Total Purchase: $3,369.55
9. Corrected total is $3,255.55
   ($3,369.55 − $114.00)
10.

Valley Kitchen Supplies

Item #	Description	Quantity	Cost/Per	Amount
D8273	sauce pans	22	$ 8.89	$195.58
E0938	Knives	16	14.99	239.84
B2902	tea pots	9	11.25	101.25
Z1298	coffee maker	4	24.50	98.00

Total Purchase: $634.67

Multiplying by Three Digits
Pages 120–121

1. 21,296; 46,292; 108,630; 213,072; 295,447
2. $20,792; 20,374; 69,438; $89,060; 273,896
3. 407,407; 253,872; 239,096; 390,750; $509,172
4.

a) Item	Estimate	b) Correct Amount
Lawn Mower	$60,000	as given
Lawn Furniture	$100,000	$97,495
Microwave Oven	$80,000	$83,439
Dishwasher	$40,000	as given
Kitchen Table	$30,000	as given
Couch & Love Seat	$280,000	as given
27-inch TV	$360,000	$368,594

Shortcuts in Multiplication
Page 122

1. 3,460; $7,560   **4.** 12,875; $16,642
2. $20,280; 49,500   **5.** 58,581; $67,089
3. 91,680; 110,010   **6.** 191,845; 339,822

Multiplying Three Numbers
Page 123

1. 378, 728, $30.00
2. 4,760; $302.40; $900.00

3. a) $94.80
   b) $142.08
   c) $234.72
   d) $1,088.64

On the Job
Page 125

1.

	Bills	Value
2	$50 bills	$100
8	$20 bills	$160
13	$10 bills	$130
19	$ 5 bills	$ 95
24	$ 1 bills	$ 24
	Total Value:	**$509**

2.

	Coins	Value
7	50¢ pieces	$3.50
15	quarters	$3.75
37	dimes	$3.70
19	nickels	$0.95
11	pennies	$0.11
	Total Value:	**$12.01**

3.

Cash Receipts Record			
Number	Total	Number	Total
$50 _2_	$ _100_	50¢ _18_	$ _9.00_
$20 _12_	$ _240_	25¢ _29_	$ _7.25_
$10 _27_	$ _270_	10¢ _33_	$ _3.30_
$5 _35_	$ _175_	5¢ _21_	$ _1.05_
$2 ___	$ ___	1¢ _14_	$ _0.14_
$1 _21_	$ _21_		

Total Bills: $ _806_ Total Coins: $ _20.74_
Total Cash Receipts: $ _826.74_
(bills + coins)

Skill Review
Page 127

1. a) Total Bills: $625
      Total Coins: $12.65
  b) & **c)**, **2–4** on deposit slip below.

FOR DEPOSIT TO THE ACCOUNT OF	CASH	CURRENCY	625	00	036
GARCIA'S FURNITURE STORE		COIN	12	65	
1843 Maple Drive	LIST CHECKS				24-7938/3239
Chicago, Illinois	12-24		125	00	
DATE _June 14_ 19—	14-32		300	00	
	26-93		225	00	
DEPOSITS MAY NOT BE AVAILABLE FOR IMMEDIATE WITHDRAWAL	TOTAL FROM OTHER SIDE				
	TOTAL		1,287	65	USE OTHER SIDE FOR ADDITIONAL LISTING
SIGN HERE FOR LESS CASH IN TELLER'S PRESENCE	LESS CASH RECEIVED				
BETTER BUSINESS BANK	CHICAGO BRANCH 2078 Michigan Avenue Chicago, Illinois	NET DEPOSIT	1,287	65	BE SURE EACH ITEM IS PROPERLY ENDORSED
⑆323070880⑆04 0833515⑈					

Unit Five: Division
Dividing
Pages 130–133

1. 12 ÷ 3 = 4 or $3\overline{)12}$ with quotient 4

2. 16 ÷ 4 = 4 or $4\overline{)16}$ with quotient 4

3. 3, 3	**12.** 7, 9	**21.** 7, 6, 6, 9, 8
4. 9, 7	**13.** 4	**22.** 3, 7, 3, 3, 5
5. 8, 4	**14.** 6	**23.** 9, 9, 8, 7, 9
6. 6, 9	**15.** 6	**24.** 8, 7, 7, 6, 6
7. 9, 8	**16.** 5	**25.** 9, 8, 4, 9, 8
8. 4, 6	**17.** 9	**26.** c
9. 8, 7	**18.** 5	**27.** a
10. 6, 7	**19.** 9	**28.** b
11. 8, 8	**20.** 8	**29.** b
		30. c

Remainders in Division
Page 134

1. 1 r 3, 1 r 2, 2 r 2, 5 r 2, 8 r 4
2. 2 r 1, 1 r 4, 2 r 2, 2 r 1, 1 r 2

Deciding What to Do with a Remainder
Page 135

1. 18 ÷ 5 = 3 r 3
   4 trips
2. 60 ÷ 9 = 6 r 6
   6 customers

3. 18 ÷ 4 = 4 r 2
   4 skirts
4. 34 ÷ 6 = 5 r 4
   6 boxes

Focus on Calculators
Pages 136–137

1. dividend: 377, divisor: 13
   Ⓒ③⑦⑦÷①③⑳
2. dividend: $7.98, divisor: 6
   Ⓒ⑦·⑨⑧÷⑥⑳
3. 38, 21, $4.53
4. 32, 34, $8.66
5. 17, 25, $1.51

6. 39, 35, $5.78
7. a) $4.89
   b) $8.78
   c) $1.29
   d) $2.79
   e) $14.35
   f) $12.49

Calculators and Remainders
Page 139

1. c
2. a
3. Rock: 118, Fill Dirt: 243, Topsoil: 32,
   Total Number of Trips: 393
4. a, d, and f are incorrect.

Dividing by One Digit
Page 141–142

1. 13 r 3, 14, 27 r 2, 26, 43 r 2
2. 13¢, 14, $15, 15, 18
3. 23, 87, 94, $54, 37
4. 16 r 1, 12 r 3, 12 r 1, 16 r 4, 12 r 3
5. 48 r 1, 47 r 2, 47 r 2, 62 r 7, 56 r 4
6. **a)** 125 **b)** 89 **c)** 115 **d)** 246
7. **a)** 63 **b)** 57 **c)** 59
8. c
9. a

In Your Life
Page 143

George: 162   Dottie: 175   Paul: 159
Harry: 178   Helen: 128   Mario: 179

Dividing into Larger Numbers
Page 145

1. 124, 163, 239, 253, 464
2. 156, $148, 243, 119, $111
3. 633, 877, $355, 687, 289
4. 147 r 1, 148 r 3, 135 r 3, 287 r 2, 385 r 3
5. 174 r 3, 124 r 5, 171 r 1, 442 r 1, 587 r 3

Using Zero as a Place Holder
Page 146

1. 90   3. 70   5. 304   7. 907
2. 700   4. $15,000   6. $903   8. 2,009

On the Job
Page 147

A. 1. 531
    2. 589
    3. 521
    4. 497
    5. 481

B. The largest number of employees you can have and still make a profit is 7.

Dividing Dollars and Cents
Page 148

1. $0.43   4. $1.32   7. $0.07   10. $0.06
2. $3.10   5. $2.01   8. $0.06   11. $0.09
3. $0.51   6. $3.22   9. $0.08   12. $0.09

In Your Life
Page 149

1. **a)** $1.13
    b) $1.09 *Best buy
    c) $1.19
2. **d)** $0.42
    e) $0.39
    f) $0.37 *Best buy

Dividing and Estimating
Page 151

1. 80, 100
2. 200, $30.00
3. 100, $2.00
4. 500, $80.00
5. Incorrect answers: Olives at $0.49 per ounce, Chicken at $2.09 per pound, and Cheese at $3.34 per pound

Estimating with Larger Divisors
Pages 152–153

1. b   4. c   7. 20, 40, $20
2. a   5. c   8. 400, 500, $200
3. b   6. a   9. 80, 20, 40

On the Job
Pages 154–155

1.

Item	Estimated Supply	To Order Yes	No
Dictionaries	2	X	
World Almanacs	5		X
Colored Markers	2	X	
Paper Glue	10		X
Typing Paper	10		X
Typewriters	5		X
Desk Chairs	2	X	

2.

Item	Estimated Unit Cost
Calculators	$5.00
Earth Globes	$20.00
File Cabinets	$80.00
Slide Projectors	$30.00
Pencil Sharpeners	$5.00
Staplers	$4.00
Computer Printers	$400.00

3. **a)** 2,000 hours   **b)** $7.00 per hour

Dividing by a Two-Digit Number
Pages 157–158

1. 3   6 8
  2, 4, 5, 9
2. 9   8
  7, 8, $0.07, $0.09
3. 6   4   4
  17, 23, 17, $0.25
4. 2 r 5, 5 r 4, 17, 34, $6.79
5. 4, $6, 5, 7, $0.50
6. 27, 21, 18, $125, $4.89
7. 5 r 4, 3 r 23, 7 r 24, 14 r 8, 20 r 27
8. 88 r 13, 118 r 20, 125 r 51, 159 r 8, 448 r 25
9. **a)** $3,425.50
  b) $2,625.00
  c) $2,158.75

On the Job
Page 159

	Vehicle Number	Monthly Miles	Gas Mileage
1.	C48	2,088	29
2.	C53	1,664	26
3.	C79	2,697	31
4.	T77	735	15
5.	T93	338	13

Shortcuts in Division
Pages 160–161

1. 2, 4, 55
2. $4, 4, 6, 7, 40
3. 4, 3, 4, $3, 18
4. 20, 90, $50, 100, 70
5. 8, $35, 70

6. 4, $50, 234
7. 6, $14, 72
8. a
9. b
10. b

Skill Review
Pages 162–163

Item	Monthly Fixed Costs
Rent	$385.00
Car Payment	$185.40
Health Insurance	$ 79.20
Car Insurance	$ 39.80
Property Insurance	$ 17.50
Total:	**$706.90**

2.

Item	3-Month Total	Average Monthly Variable Costs
Electric Power	$68.55	$ 22.85
Gas, Heat, etc.	$116.40	$ 38.80
Car Gas & Oil	$177.75	$ 59.25
Clothes	$231.60	$ 77.20
Food	$563.25	$187.75
Entertainment	$162.00	$ 54.00
	Total:	**$439.85**

3. $1,146.75 ($706.90 + $439.85)
4. $336.05 ($1,482.80 − $1,146.75)
5. a) $10,150 ($11,150 − $1,000)
   b) Estimate: $200

Unit Six: Measurement of Time

Reading a Clock
Page 166

Answers may vary slightly with reading of the minute hands.

1. 9:00
2. 6:30
3. 2:26
4. 11:05
5. 11:55
6. 4:38

Finding Earlier and Later Times
Page 168

1. 10:25
2. 7:40
3. 2:50
4. 12:40

5. Monday: 8 hr. 30 min.
   Tuesday: 7 hr. 45 min.
   Wednesday: 6 hr. 40 min.

In Your Life
Page 169

1. 20 minutes
2. 17 minutes
3. 9:41
4. 28 minutes

On the Job
Page 171
Computing Weekly Pay

Answers 1 & 2

Monday:	7 hr.	45 min.
Tuesday:	9 hr.	30 min.
Wednesday:	8 hr.	15 min.
Thursday:	7 hr.	30 min.
Friday:	8 hr.	
Saturday:	3 hr.	30 min.
Total Time for Week:	42 hr. 150 min.	
	= 44 hr. 30 min.	

$$\begin{array}{r} 2 \text{ hr. } 30 \text{ min.} \\ 60\overline{)150} \\ -\underline{120} \\ 30 \end{array}$$

3. Total Regular Hours: 40 hours
   Total Overtime Hours: 4 hours 30 minutes
4. Total Regular Pay: $280.00 ($7.00 × 40)
   Total Overtime Pay: $47.25
   ($10.50 × 4 plus $5.25)
   Total Gross Pay: $327.25
   ($280.00 + $47.25)

On the Job
Pages 172–173
Using a Calculator

1. 18
2. $1,170
3. $68.25
4.

JUNE						
SUN.	MON.	TUE.	WED.	THUR.	FRI.	SAT.
				1	2	3
4	5	6	7	8	9	10
11	12	*office meeting 9:00 A.M.* 13	14	15	16	*6 hrs. overtime* 17
Rose's Birthday 18	19	20	21	22	23	24
25	26	27	28	29	30	

5. 19 days

6. a) 180 regular hours
    b) $1,170.00 (180 × $6.50)
    c) $58.50 ($9.75 × 6)
    d) $1,228.50 ($1,170.00 + $58.50)

In Your Life
Page 174

1. 3:00 P.M. (2 hours earlier)
2. 8:30 A.M. (2 hours later)
3. 2:45 P.M. (1 hour later)
4. 5:30 P.M. eastern standard time.
She arrived in Philadelphia at 2:30 P.M. Seattle time. Philadelphia time is 3 hours later, or 5:30 P.M.

Post-test
Pages 175–180

1. 7986
2. Drawer C
3. $4,280.12, $4,190.00, $1,876.90, $114.08

4.

RICARDO'S			
Item	Quantity	Unit Price	Total Cost
Plain Doughnut	2	$.37	$.74
Jumbo Doughnut	1	.62	.62
Large Coffee	1	.92	.92
		Subtotal	$2.28
		Tax	.14
		Total	$2.42

5. 3 pennies, 1 nickel, 2 quarters, 2 $1 bills

6.

RICARDO'S			
Item	Quantity	Unit Price	Total Cost
Cholesterol-Free Doughnut	1	$.50	$.50
Small Coffee	1	.59	.59
Large Coffee	1	.92	.92
		Subtotal	$2.01
		Tax	.14
		Total	$2.15

7. 1 dime, 3 quarters
8. $2

9.–11.   Account #ED98721

RECORD ALL CHARGES OR CREDITS THAT AFFECT YOUR ACCOUNT

NUMBER	DATE	DESCRIPTION OF TRANSACTION	PAYMENT /DEBIT (−)	√ T	FEE (IF ANY) (−)	DEPOSIT /CREDIT (+)	BALANCE $557 90
211	9/18	Big W. Grocery	$93.15	$	$		93 15
							464 75
	9/18	machine withdrawal	20.00				20 00
							444 75
212	9/21	Alfredo Davis	400.00				400 00
							44 75
	9/22	paycheck deposit				419.57	419 57
							464 32
213	9/25	Southwest Electric	31.17				31 17
							433 15
214	9/27	Corner Currency	50.15				50 15
							383 00
	9/27	rebate				9.80	9 80
							392 80

12. Andy's chocolates: 1,300
Crunchers candy: 1,200
Evertop batteries: 72
Flavorite bubble gum: 8,400
Flavorite gum: 6,720
pocket pens: 150
three-layer bars: 600

13. 4,800
14. $3,875.00
15. 15
16. 8-ounce can: $0.14 per ounce
12-ounce can: $0.13 per ounce * best value
16-ounce can: $0.14 per ounce
17. 10-ounce can: $0.07 per ounce
12-ounce can: $0.06 per ounce * best value
16-ounce can: $0.07 per ounce
18. $6.24
19. $3.36 − $2.88 = $0.48
20. Estimate: $16 ÷ 8 = $2;
$16.21 ÷ 8 = $2.03
21. electricity: $22
gas heat: $44
gas and oil for car: $40
food: $365
clothing: $55
22. $2,285 per month
23. $62.50
24. $1,160 (fixed + variable)
25. $1,125
26. 15 minutes
27. #160
28. 55 minutes